Abbreviations

<u>Used in the Text</u>

AFF	Army Field Forces
AWC	Army War College
BG	Brigadier General
CAC	Combined Arms Center
CONARC	Continental Army Command
CGSC	Command and General Staff College
CSA	Chief of Staff of the Army
CSI	Combat Studies Institute
DOD	Department of Defense
FORSCOM	Force Command
GEN	General
JCS	Joint Chiefs of Staff
LAM	Louisiana Maneuvers
LIC	Low-Intensity Conflict
LTG	Lieutenant General
NATO	North Atlantic Treaty Organization
NSC	National Security Council
QDR	Quadrennial Defense Review
SACEUR	Supreme Allied Commander, Europe
SAMS	School of Advanced Military Studies
SSI	Strategic Studies Institute
TRADOC	Training and Doctrine Command
VCSA	Vice Chief of Staff of the Army

<u>Used in the Notes</u>

DDEL	Dwight D. Eisenhower Library
DDEP	Papers of Dwight D. Eisenhower
OSA for NSA	Office of the Special Assistant for National Security Affairs
WHO	White House Office
DDRS	Declassified Documents Retrieval System
HJCS	*History of the Joint Chiefs of Staff*
HOSD	*History of the Office of the Secretary of Defense*
NARA	National Archives and Records Administration, College Park
NSC	National Security Council
RG	Record Group (at NARA)

Contents

Contents (cont'd)

iii

Introduction

The danger is not that we shall read the signals and indicators with too little skill; the danger is a poverty of expectations, a routine obsession with a few dangers that may be familiar rather than likely.

–Thomas Schelling

In his foreword to Roberta Wohlstetter's Bancroft prize-winning book *Pearl Harbor* (1962), Thomas Schelling addressed the problem faced by a government in foreseeing and anticipating future contingencies. For Schelling, Wohlstetter had demonstrated that the failure of the US government was not in its provision of sufficient warning of the coming attack, but in a culture of strategic analysis which was preoccupied with what the Japanese would *obviously* do rather than the full range of choices and actions at their disposal.[1] The question of how the United States could best prepare itself for future threats and shape its military establishment to attain a balance between near-term operational demands and long-term force transformation were topics of considerable interest even before the attacks of 11 September 2001 reoriented the policy of the current administration towards what has come to be known as the Global War on Terror. Indeed, since the end of the Cold War the size of the US military establishment and the utility of military force were hotly debated topics. Like many other periods in American history, the US government and people had hoped that the end of the Cold War confrontation with the Soviet Union would provide a "peace dividend" and allow national resources to be reoriented towards a wide array of domestic concerns. While the defense budget was trimmed accordingly, however, the US military soon found itself deployed overseas for a multitude of wide-ranging operations at a tempo which greatly taxed its personnel and increasingly deferred plans for modernization of the force. When the administration of George W. Bush assumed office in January 2001, there was a strong sense that the United States was still struggling to find a proper strategic orientation for the post-Cold War world. The Bush administration undertook the strategic review characteristic of any new administration, one that had additional importance given a Congressionally-mandated Quadrennial Review Report on Defense was expected from the Department of Defense during 2001. That summer, Schelling's phrase about the "poverty of expectations" gained currency amongst the ranks of senior Pentagon officials who gave it widespread circulation.[2] In its use was an implicit criticism of the type of force planning and strategic thinking which had characterized preceding administrations' approaches to defense.

To a larger extent, the dilemmas about the utility of force and the proper size of the American military have always existed. After World War II, as the United States awoke to its global role, the defense establishment grew to a size and scope well-beyond anything the American people had hitherto been comfortable with in peacetime. Even when the Cold War grew hot in places like Korea and Vietnam, the United States maintained a balance between guns and butter. It is in determining that balance that debates about the nature and scale of the US military have continued ever since. The debate always grows particularly acute in periods of relative peace after the end of periods of extended conflict. The object of this study is to determine the ways by which the US Army, through internal or external initiatives or pressure, has adapted to perceived needs of the future through the impact of recent or past experience. Three episodes in the Army's history since the Second World War are examined. The three periods examined in this study are the decade after the Korean War, the Vietnam War, and the end of the Cold War. In each of these periods a number of factors pertinent to Army "lessons learning," modernization, and transformation will be touched on to provide a framework for the broader discussion of how the Army has gone about anticipating its future use within the framework of US national security policy.[3] These factors will include doctrine, organization (primarily through the lens of the divisional unit), training, and education.[4] This study will seek to determine if the Army has proclivities which favor certain modes over others, and assess which have been more effective agents for change. In addition, the study will take account of the Army's response to stimuli, such as changes in technology, national strategy, and congressionally mandated change.

Public attention toward roles and missions of the armed forces increased markedly in the later 1940s, due in large part to the well-publicized service debates over resources. While the Army was hardly a neutral observer in these debates, the discussions over defense unification particularly highlighted splits between the newly minted Air Force and the Navy, climaxing in the 1949 "revolt of the admirals." The massive rearmament program which followed US intervention in the Korean War muted this debate for some years. Once the Korean Armistice set in, a new round of debates over roles, missions, and US Cold War strategy began anew. In this incarnation the Army was to assume an ever growing role in the controversy. In the three periods assessed in this study, the role of the

2

executive branch, Congress, and the public all increased over time, adding numerous voices to the debates about how Army adaptation should proceed. After the especially contentious US involvement in Vietnam, the notion of learning lessons from past experiences gained greater currency in debates, both within the Army and in the wider public. Before turning to these three eras of adaptation, a brief survey of the US Army from World War II to the Korean War is in order.

The Post-World War II Army

Russell Weigley has written that "the historic preoccupation of the Army's thought in peacetime has been the manpower question: how, in an unmilitary nation, to muster adequate numbers of capable soldiers quickly should war occur. At the close of World War II the Army's thoughts about its role and mission returned to that historic preoccupation."[5] During the contentious service debates over roles and missions which raged during 1948-49, the Army often seemed to be sitting on the sidelines as the Air Force and Navy debated who should have control over atomic weapons. In the *Functions of the Armed Services Papers* in 1948, the Army retained primary responsibility for organizing, training, and equipping forces for sustained combat on land.[6] As late as 1950, the Army was "shaped less by military doctrine looking to a future war, to which this Army often seemed so irrelevant, than by the past, by the last war, of whose massive armies it was the remnant."[7] Robert Doughty concurs with this assessment in his study, arguing that by 1950 army tactical doctrine "effectively remained that of World War II."[8]

In the midst of World War II the Army launched a massive historical account of its wartime experience. In July 1943 the US Army established a Historical Branch to document the Army's World War II experience.[9] The Historical Branch was subsequently assigned to the War Department Special Staff, where it became known as the Historical Division and placed under the command of a general officer. There a plan was conceived for a multi-volume "official" history of the Army's participation in the Second World War. The project was to be of considerable length to provide a "great deal of detail that the Army itself needed for educational purposes."[10] The Historical Division began production of the series *The United States Army in World War II*, better known today as the Green Books. Complementing this effort, the European Theater of Operations, Historical Division created an Operational History (German) Section in January 1946 to "exploit enemy experiences" of German general officers who were then prisoners of war.[11] The material collected, combined with captured German records, produced a flood of material. Its collection and dissemination was encouraged by both Generals Eisenhower and Bradley during their respective tenures as Army Chief of Staff. General Bradley authorized the addition of a Foreign Studies Branch to the Historical Division in December 1948.[12] It was initially headed by BG Paul Robinett. He reported in April 1949 that 721 German studies of "current and future use to the staff and schools" had been translated.[13] After World War II the Army also conducted a wide ranging review of a great number of issues when the European Theater of Operations convened a General Board. But in the flush of victory after World War II, with the rush to demobilize and bring the boys home, the process of assessing performance and adapting to future roles initially merited little public attention.

One of the subjects reviewed by the European Theater of Operations' General Board was the organization of the Army's divisional structures.[14] These reports and recommendations from conferences on armor and infantry were forwarded by Chief of Army Ground Forces Jacob Devers to the General Staff in July 1946. Though Army Chief of Staff Dwight Eisenhower initially felt these recommendations called for units that were too large and inflexible, he found little support for his views from a board of senior advisors that he asked to review the recommendations. Eisenhower would remain a persistent critic of larger divisions throughout his tenure as Chief of Staff and as NATO's Supreme Allied Commander, Europe.[15] By 1948 the divisional structures were codified, reflecting the optimal divisions of World War II. The new infantry division was to have 18,804 officers and men organized into three regiments of three battalions each of infantry. In addition, the division was supplemented by independent tank and antiaircraft artillery battalions, as well as tank companies assigned to each infantry regiment for support. The armored division retained its general 1943 light structure. It was made up of 15,973 officers and men with three medium tank battalions, three armored infantry battalions, and three 105-mm howitzer battalions, supported by a heavy tank battalion, and an antiaircraft artillery battalion. Because of funding and manpower shortages, however, only one of the Army's ten postwar divisions (1st Infantry Division in Germany) attained full strength. The remainder of these divisions were considerably below strength, typically ranging from 12,500 to 13,650 officers and men.

In the years after World War II the Army underwent massive demobilization and reduction.[16] The Army that remained after demobilization was heavily engaged in occupation duties in Japan, Germany, and Austria. The advent of the nuclear age; the development of the Air Force as an independent military branch; the challenge of military unification; and declining defense budgets served to occupy much of the Army's attention in this period. Deteriorating relations with the Soviet Union increasingly preoccupied strategic planning by 1947-48. The subsequent Berlin Crisis further galvanized US attention towards a potential confrontation with the Soviets. In response to this dawning Cold War, the US military establishment, especially the newly independent Air Force, increasingly focused its attention on the application of the US atomic power to a future war.

By 1950 the Army was scaled back to 10 under-strength divisions with 591,000 men in the active component. Of these, there were four infantry divisions serving as occupation forces in Japan and the lone 1st Infantry Division was in Germany. The remaining five divisions (2 airborne, 2 infantry, and 1 armored) served as a mobile reserve in the United States.[17] However, US emergency war plans prior to 1950 were geared for the rapid evacuation of US forces overseas in the event of a war with the Soviets. The Army's primary role in a future war—along with that of the US Navy—seemed to primarily be to hold on to valuable real-estate from which long-range bomber attacks could be launched against the Soviet Union.[18] Occupation duties and funding deficiencies further limited training time, which greatly reduced the readiness of the Army's divisions to engage in hostilities in any event.[19]

The outbreak of the Korean War in June 1950 initially served as a rude shock to the Army and to the United States.[20] It also provided the opportunity for the Army to again prove its mettle and provided an impetus for a major increase in US defense spending. According to Russell Weigley, the Korean War—by engendering the Army with a new sense of purpose—"made possible a sort of Army renaissance."[21] The improved budgetary position of all the services following the outbreak of the Korean War contributed to a considerable buildup of US conventional forces. This buildup had an impact on the Army well beyond the Korean battlefield. Prior to Korea the services had been engaged in a protracted fight for resources under Truman's $13.5 billion budget ceiling for defense spending for FY 1951. Following the outbreak of Korea, however, the fiscal restraint which had hitherto characterized the Truman administration's approach to defense went out the window. By December 1950 supplemental appropriations had been requested of and approved by Congress that brought defense spending up to $48.2 billion.[22] On the policy level, the US government's Cold War outlook was shaped by NSC 68, a document which had been drafted before the outbreak of the Korean War, but whose implementation as policy resulted from the mood in Washington after the war broke out.[23] The Army that emerged by the end of the Korean War reflected this considerable expansion.[24]

Overview

With the advent of the Eisenhower administration, however, retrenchment of forces again provoked serious concern in the Army Staff. In December 1954, Army strength stood at 17 divisions and 1,404,600 men on active duty. Only six of these divisions were deployed in the Far East, another five had been sent to Europe as part of the NATO buildup, and the remaining six were in the United States. But in FY 1956, the Eisenhower administration requested $7.3 billion for the Army, a decrease of nearly $5 billion from Truman's FY 1954 budget. Not only was this a net decline of considerable magnitude, but the Army's slice of the defense pie dropped from 33.7 % in FY 1954 to 24.8% in FY 1956.[25] By the end of the Eisenhower administration, active duty Army strength stood at about 870,000 men.[26] The Army would go through a similar reduction in manpower as US involvement in Vietnam wound down. Between 1969 and 1975, Army end strength fell from nearly 1.5 million to 780,000 men. At the end of the Cold War, end strength again declined precipitously, falling from 780,000 men to 475,000 between 1987 and 1993. The Army's share of the defense budget again dropped from 30% in 1991 to 23% in 1996.[27] Changes in manpower, budgetary allocation, and sometimes the strategic environment itself characterize the periods which follow periods of extended conflict and/or confrontation. Understanding how the Army has adapted in the past is instructive when looking ahead to a future period of adaptation.

While it is unclear how long US forces will remain committed to operations in Afghanistan and Iraq, it is reasonable to suggest that the Army will soon find itself facing yet another period of adapting itself after a period of prolonged conflict. Indeed, LTG Peter Chiarelli has recently written that, "given our Nation's inconsistent track record when reorganizing its forces following periods of national crisis, the time is now to start discussing how the military and interagency organizations that emerge from Iraq and Afghanistan will prepare for a dangerous future."[28] The US Army has faced a similar challenge many times before in its long history. This study will recount the three attempts to adapt in the last half of the 20th century, and analyze the strengths and weaknesses of past Army adaptation.

Notes

1. Roberta Wohlstetter, *Pearl Harbor: Warning and Decision* (Stanford, CA: Stanford University Press, 1962), p.vii. The book won the Bancroft Prize in 1963.

2. This phrase was used by both Deputy Secretary of Defense Paul Wolfowitz and Secretary of Defense Donald Rumsfeld during the summer and fall of 2001. The earliest use I have come across was in Wolfowitz's Commencement Address at the US Military Academy, West Point on 2 June 2001. Available at: http://www.defenselink.mil/speeches/speech.aspx?speechid=363. Rumsfeld subsequently used the phrase in his testimony to the House and Senate Armed Services Committees on 20 June 2001. Senate Armed Services Committee, *Hearing on U.S. National Security Strategy*, 21 June 2001, pp.4-5. Chaired by Senator Carl Levin (D-MI). Retrieved from LexisNexis Congressional Search. Rumsfeld made similar remarks to the House Armed Services Committee later that day. Available at: http://commdocs.house.gov/committees/security/has172000.000/has172000_0.HTM. Bob Woodward recounts that Rumsfeld's "routinely handed out or recommended a book called *Pearl Harbor: Warning and Decision* by Roberta Wohlstetter. Rumsfeld particularly recommended the foreword." Bob Woodward, *Bush at War* (New York: Simon and Schuster Paperbacks, 2002), p.22.

3. For a stimulating discussion of this problem in an earlier era, see Antulio J. Echevarria II, *Imagining Future War: The West's Technological Revolution and Visions of Wars to Come, 1880-1914* (Westport, CT: Praeger Security International, 2007).

4. With regard to Army doctrine, this study will confine itself primarily to the discussion of FM 100-5, which since 1976 at least has been referred to as the capstone/keystone Army doctrinal manual.

5. Russell F. Weigley, *History of the United States Army*, enlarged edition (Bloomington, IN: Indiana University Press, 1984), p.496.

6. Alice C. Cole, et. al. *The Department of Defense: Documents on Establishment and Organization 1944-1978* (Washington, DC: Historical Office, Office of the Secretary of Defense, 1978), pp.265-93, and Steven L. Rearden, *History of the Office of the Secretary of Defense*, vol.I: *The Formative Years 1947-1950* (Washington, DC: Historical Office, Office of the Secretary of Defense, 1984), p.395 92 [hereafter *HOSD*].

7. Weigley, *History of the United States Army*, enlarged edition, p.502.

8. Robert A. Doughty, *The Evolution of US Army Tactical Doctrine, 1946-76* (Fort Leavenworth, KS: Combat Studies Institute, 2001, reprint of 1979 edition), p.6.

9. For the Army's appreciation of the need to carry out historical study arising from its World War II experience, see Stetson Conn, *Historical Work in the United States Army, 1862-1954* (Washington, DC: United States Army, Center

of Military History, 1980); Paul M. Robinett, "The Exploitation of History by the United States Army," *Military Review*, v.34 (December 1954), pp.11-13; and Kevin Soutor, "To Stem the Red Tide: The German Report Series and Its Effect on American Defense Doctrine, 1948-1954," *The Journal of Military History*, v.57, n.4 (October 1993), pp.653-688.

10. Conn, *Historical Work in the United States Army, 1862-1954*, p.116.

11. Soutor, "To Stem the Red Tide," p.659.

12. Conn, *Historical Work in the United States Army, 1862-1954*, p.182.

13. Quoted in Conn, *Historical Work in the United States Army, 1862-1954*, p.182

14. John B. Wilson, *Maneuver and Firepower: The Evolution of Divisions and Separate Brigades* (Washington, DC: Center of Military History, United States Army, 1998), pp.222-29.

15. Wilson, *Maneuver and Firepower*, p.225. An Eisenhower memorandum for SHAPE Chief of Staff General Al Gruenther in September 1951 stated, "As you know, I have felt the typical American division is far too expensive in personnel . . . ," Louis Galambos, ed. *The Papers of Dwight David Eisenhower*, vol.XII: *NATO and the Campaign of 1952* (Baltimore, MD: the Johns Hopkins University Press, 1989), p.569.

16. See John C. Sparrow, *History of Personnel Demobilization in the United States Army* (Washington, DC: Center of Military History, facsimile edition, 1994).

17. Richard W. Stewart, gen. ed., *American Military History*, v.II: *The United States Army in a Global Era, 1917-2003* (Washington, DC: Center of Military History, 2005), p.211.

18. There was a degree of unreality to these plans, as the Air Force before the Korean War expansion was ill-prepared to launch the war-ending campaigns they claimed. On the Air Force, see Harry R. Borowski, *A Hollow Threat: Air Power and Containment before Korea* (Westport, CT: Greenwood Press, 1982); and Michael S. Sherry, *The Rise of American Air Power: The Creation of Armageddon* (New Haven, CT: Yale University Press, 1987). On the Navy's conception of its role, see Michael Palmer, *Origins of the Maritime Strategy: The Development of American Naval Strategy 1945-1955* (Annapolis, MD: Naval Institute Press, 1988).

19. *Field Service Regulations-Operations, FM 100-5* (Washington, DC: US GPO, August 1949), pp.256-63, *Sixty Years of Reorganizing for Combat: A Historical Trend Analysis*, CSI Report No.14 (Fort Leavenworth, KS: Combat Studies Institute, 1999), pp.14-16, and John J. McGrath, *The Brigade: A History, Its Organization and Employment in the US Army* (Fort Leavenworth, KS: Combat Studies Institute, 2004), pp.46-50.

20. William Stueck, *The Korean War: An International History* (Princeton, NJ: Princeton University Press, 1995), pp.10-11. On the unpreparedness of US troops

in their first major engagement of the war, see Roy K. Flint, "Task Force Smith and the 24th Division: Delay and Withdrawal, 5-19 July 1950," in *America's First Battles*, ed. by Charles E. Heller and William A. Stofft (Lawrence, KS: University Press of Kansas, 1986), pp.266-99. For an extended analysis, see Thomas E. Hanson, "America's First Cold War Army: Combat Readiness in the Eighth U.S. Army, 1949-1950" (PhD Dissertation, Ohio State University, 2006).

21. Weigley, *History of the United States Army*, enlarged edition, p.525.

22. Doris M. Condit, *History of the Office of the Secretary of Defense*, v.II: *The Test of War 1950-1953* (Washington, DC: Historical Office, Office of the Secretary of Defense, 1988), pp.223-42.

23. A copy of the document can be found in *Foreign Relations of the United States* [hereafter *FRUS*], *1950*, vol.1, pp.235-92. On interpretations of the document, see Ernest R. May, ed., *American Cold War Strategy: Interpreting NSC 68* (Boston, MA: Bedford Books, 1993). Melvin Leffler argues that NSC 68 was no radical departure, but rather a continuation of the "assumptions that had been driving U.S. foreign policy during the Truman administration." For the continuity argument, see Melvin Leffler, A *Preponderance of Power: National Security, the Truman administration, and the Cold War* (Stanford, CA: Stanford University Press, 1992), pp.355-360. Paul Nitze, the primary author of NSC 68, takes a similar tack in his own account, see *From Hiroshima to Glasnost: At the Center of Decision, A Memoir* (New York: Grove Weidenfeld, 1989), pp.93-98.

24. On the Army's use of NSC 68 to advance its institutional agenda, see David T. Fautua, "The 'Long Pull' Army: NSC 68, the Korean War, and the Creation of the Cold War U.S. Army," *The Journal of Military History*, v.61, n.1 (January 1997), pp.93-120.

25. Watson, *HOSD*, v.IV: *Into the Missile Age, 1956-1960*, p.32.

26. Linn, *The Echo of Battle*, p.165.

27. David McCormick, *The Downsized Warrior: America's Army in Transition* (New York: New York University Press, 1998), pp.11, 26.

28. Peter W. Chiarelli, with Stephen M. Smith, "Learning From Our Modern Wars," *Military Review*, v.LXXXVII, n.5 (September-October 2007), p.15.

Chapter 1
The Pentomic Era

The intensification of the Cold War and the military buildup during the Korean War led to a greatly accelerated atomic weapons development and production in the United States. The massive growth of the atomic arsenal in the 1950s on the one hand made it possible for the Air Force's Strategic Air Command to plan the sort of decisive use of air power that air power theorists had once only envisioned. At the same time it raised questions about whether or not the obliteration of entire cities was the proper conduct for future war.[1] The emphasis on nuclear weapons and air power in the early Cold War made many question whether or not land warfare had become obsolete. While Korea had demonstrated that land combat still had a place, the desire in the US to avoid future wars of the same ilk as Korea further reinforced conceptions in the early Eisenhower era that the Army's traditional place in American defense was being badly undermined by revolutionary changes in warfare. The critique of traditional notions of warfare and the roll of Army professionals created a profound conceptual challenge with which the Army struggled throughout the Eisenhower era.[2]

In the late 1950s the Army briefly experimented with a divisional design grouped around five nominally independent battle groups. Dubbed the "Pentomic" division by then US Army Chief of Staff Maxwell Taylor, this new divisional design was the most striking attempt by the Army to adapt itself to the strategic climate of the era of massive retaliation. The concept was short-lived, however. It has been widely remembered primarily as a failed adaptation of the post-World War II Army.[3] The Army's perception of much of the Eisenhower presidency was one of frustration. Successive Chiefs of Staff Matthew Ridgway and Maxwell Taylor became engaged in a largely unsuccessful effort to convince the Eisenhower administration to alter the provisions of its New Look national security policy. Though Ridgway and Taylor applied different tactics, they both sought to meet the Soviet challenge through an application of US strength that did not rely, as they and the Army perceived it, so exclusively on strategic air power.

The eventual short-lived adoption of the Pentomic division structure was a facet of the Army's attempts to cope with its perception of the challenge presented by the nuclear age. Curriculum changes in the Army school system late in the decade also reflected the Army's attempt to come to terms with the New Look. During this period the Army also undertook significant changes in its organizational structure. The creation of the Continental Army Command (CONARC) in 1955, which harkened back to the wartime Army Ground Forces system, considerably outlasted the Pentomic divisional arrangement. It was perhaps the most significant reform of the post-Korean War Army.

The US Army and the Conceptual Challenge of the Nuclear Age

An attempt was made by the Army's educational system to deal with the challenges posed by the nature of warfare in the atomic age. Before proceeding with a discussion of how this developed, a brief review of Army education in the postwar era is in order. The Army's views on postwar education for the armed forces were initially strongly influenced by the War Department Military Education Board's (Gerow Board) recommendations of 1946. These had called for a systematic, hierarchic approach to officer education in the Army. Officers would progress from basic to advanced branch schools, then to an Armed Forces Staff College after ten years of service, with a capstone program offered by attendance for selective officers after twenty years of service to the Industrial College of the Armed Forces or the National War College. All three of these latter phases were to be opened to officers from all three services.[4] However, before the Gerow Board recommendations could be put into effect, the recommendations were largely invalidated by the fluid situation in the armed services in the immediate postwar years.

The Army War College had ceased holding classes in the summer of 1940; courses did not resume until October 1950.[5] The War College had originally been closed because of the desperate need for qualified officers heading into the massive expansion of the US Army during World War II. After the war the Army had supported the establishment of a National War College to supplant the earlier service schools. Though the National War College was created, the Navy and newly created Air Force retained their own war colleges.[6] Thus, after World War II the US Army faced a five year period when it was bereft of a capstone educational institution. However, the Command and General Staff School remained open during the war and after to address the pressing need for staff officers. It was renamed the Command and General Staff College (CGSC) in 1947.

In 1948 the Army instructed LTG Manton S. Eddy, Commandant of Fort Leavenworth from 1948 to 1950, to undertake a study to reorganize the college in order to improve its efficiency and competitiveness in the inter-service competition for scarce defense resources. Eddy's leadership led to recommendations which "challenged the direction that Leavenworth and the Army were headed after the war."[7] They did so by stressing the need for officers who were not trained for specialized staff functions, but instead looked to the Army as a whole. Of special importance here was developing an appreciation for and understanding of the "evolutionary effects of new [atomic] weapons on warfare."[8] Eddy felt that it was critical for the Army to think about warfare in the atomic age, not just integrate lessons learned from operations in the Second World War. Two of Eddy's CGSC instructors, COL G. C. Reinhardt and LTC W. R. Kintner, produced an early book on the subject with his encouragement.[9] Despite Eddy's interest,the influence of atomic weapons on the Leavenworth curriculum was not terribly pronounced. It was not until the curricular reforms of 1957-58 that a substantial portion of the CGSC curriculum was devoted to the study of atomic warfare.[10] The Army War College, when it reopened in 1950, initially concentrated on reviewing World War II-style campaigns, though after 1952 increasing attention was given to problems of nuclear warfare. However, the "Army War College was not a major participant in the debates over the New Look, nor was it yet a major participant in the debates over innovations in weapons, tactics, and organization."[11]

Eddy was certainly not alone in pushing the Army to start thinking about the application of atomic weapons to the battlefield.[12] By 1950-51 a number of officers were advocating the development of atomic munitions for tactical employment. In the spring of 1951, Secretary of Defense George C. Marshall and Deputy Secretary of Defense Robert Lovett, while conferring with Senator Brien McMahon, agreed that there was some need for more light weight, tactical atomic weapons in the US stockpile.[13] Project VISTA at the California Institute of Technology got under way in 1951. VISTA grew out of the desire to improve air-ground coordination on the Korean battlefield, but soon morphed into a study of a future battlefield in Western Europe.[14] By late December the study conclusions were being drawn up, and by February 1952 the report was briefed several times in Washington, DC.[15] The VISTA report stressed the need to develop a tactical atomic capability. An early version of the conclusions went so far as to state that strategic atomic forces should be held in reserve as a deterrent, pre-supposing the Soviets had not launched an attack on US cities. Instead it called for the application of approximately 100 tactical weapons against forward airfields in the Soviet Union and Eastern Europe, with the intention that most of Soviet air power could be destroyed on the ground. The report saw little promise for future thermonuclear weapons on the battlefield, instead advocating the use of fission implosion weapons in the 1-5 kiloton range. While it was recognized that some troop concentrations would justify the application of tactical nuclear weapons, the report pointed out that most interdiction targets were "more suitable for conventional weapons."[16] With its reserved attitude towards SACs strategic bombing campaign, the VISTA report drew ire from the Air Force. The report was soon effectively shelved.[17] As a result, little came of VISTA initially, though its suggestions about tactical nuclear combat had long resonance. One operative recommendation put into practice was for the Army to establish a Combat Developments Group.[18]

The Army also tried to determine the impact of atomic weapons on combat by participating in the weapons testing in the Nevada desert. Exercise DESERT ROCK was conducted at Frenchman's Flat, Nevada on 1 November 1951. Its purpose was to demonstrate that troops could advance into an area after the detonation of an atomic bomb. The test involved participation of 2,000 soldiers from the III Corps and was observed by a Congressional delegation from the Joint Congressional Committee on Atomic Energy. After the exercise, the Congressional delegates issued a joint statement which stated that "Atomic bombs can be used on the battlefield to pave the way for ground advance without radiation hazard."[19] To demonstrate this to the observing troops, who were stationed about seven miles from ground zero when the detonation took place, a number of sheep were placed in underground bunkers and pillboxes. After the explosion the soldiers toured the battlefield and witnessed that the sheep were alive and unharmed.[20] The following spring, troops observed a 31-kiloton air drop from trenches located 7,000 yards from ground zero.[21] Over the next several years, several more exercises were conducted in the DESERT ROCK series.

In 1948-49 the Army began development work on an atomic artillery shell for the massive 280mm gun. The 280mm gun had begun life as a conventional artillery piece developed by the Ordnance Corps in the closing stages of World War II. Secretary of the Army Frank Pace publicly announced that the Army was developing nuclear artillery shells in May 1952, though he cautioned that there was "No indication today that warfare of the future would not present a continuing need for many of our current conventional weapons."[22] By June 1954, there were five Army 280mm gun battalions operational in Europe, joined by four Honest John rocket batteries by year's end.[23] Most Army Combat Engineer Battalions in the US and Europe were also "capable of employing atomic weapons as demolition munitions" by 1954.[24] The 280mm gun had been criticized by the VISTA report for its cumbersome size, relative immobility, and limited range of 18 miles (insufficient to reach many of the targets VISTA recommended), and indeed the Army never pressed very hard for large numbers of 280mm guns. Ultimately nuclear equipped missiles and air deliverable weapons, not artillery, predominated in the US arsenal. But Army emphasis on guided missiles would fuel inter-service rivalry later in the decade as Army missiles approached ranges that the Air Force felt intruded on its strategic bombing prerogatives.

While these developments were taking place, the Army was also engaged in fighting the ground war in Korea under the auspices of a United Nations command. As that war approached its stalemated conclusion, the Army also had to address what the Korean experience implied for future training, doctrine, and education. In a report to the National Security Council in June 1953, the Army reported improvements in doctrine and techniques for limited offensive and defensive actions as a result of the Korean combat.[25] The early reverses of the Korean War were seen as a result of the under-strength, under-equipped divisional structure of the 1945-50 period. The official Army position on lessons learned from Korea was that "no real changes in doctrine had occurred or had been necessary during the war."[26] What difficulties had been encountered in combat resulted more from the failure to implement doctrine by units who had been geared towards occupation duties instead of combat. General John R. Hodge, Chief of Army Field Forces, wrote in the bulletin *Combat Information* in May 1953:

> Although we should use caution in revising our training based on the impact of Korea, there are nevertheless many fundamental lessons we have learned in Korea, or more often relearned, that will apply regardless of the type of terrain or operation. Therefore, we can profit greatly from analyzing our deficiencies in Korean combat and placing appropriate stress on those subjects in training. Many of these deficiencies are not peculiar to Korea—they can be found in historical studies from World War I and World War II. We are still making mistakes that are 35 years old.[27]

The failures in Korea were seen as best rectified through paying closer attention to established doctrine. Training programs were to focus on inculcating lessons that the Army felt it already had learned. The post-Korea revision of FM 100-5 did stress that, "The continuing possibility of limited wars requires the maintenance in being of Army forces capable of immediate commitment."[28] This notion of an Army that was ready to fight immediately, rather than having a long-period to build itself up as had traditionally been the case in American wars, was one of the central "lessons" drawn from Korea. But it also reflected the perception of a future war with the Soviets. The Soviets were expected to launch a massive assault on Western Europe, perhaps with little or no warning, that might reach the Channel ports in as little as thirty days.[29] Since none of the NATO allies wanted to contemplate the consequences of Soviet occupation and "liberation" by the US after the air atomic campaign, there was an imperative to develop a viable and ready defense for Western Europe than had been demonstrated on the Korean Peninsula.

The implicit habit formed by using massed artillery and airpower in Korea in support of defensive operations reinforced a tendency towards "attrition at the expense of maneuver."[30] This tendency contributed to an internal Army debate which opened in the professional journals in the spring of 1953. The debate was touched off by armor officers who were concerned about the defensive mindset that had crept into Army thinking following the stalemate in Korea. MG Robert Grow, recently retired, warned of the creeping defensive mindedness in US Army thinking. He thought the Army should turn its thought towards preparing a balanced army to fight a "modern continental war." Such an army would need a strong mobile element, so he called for one out of every three US divisions to be armored, and for the proportion of US forces deployed in Europe to contain an even higher armored component.[31] General Jacob Devers, who had served as head of Army Ground Forces before his retirement in 1949, argued that the advent of atomic firepower on the battlefield would "Not eliminate armor; it will supplement and improve it, and require it for delivery." In order for armor to adapt to this future battlefield, Devers hoped that armored divisions would aim at reduced manpower and increased mobility.[32] The internal debate on offensive versus defensive thinking would soon be subsumed into the larger debate over national security policy in the Eisenhower administration.

The Army and the "New Look"

As President one of Eisenhower's first priorities was ending hostilities in the Korean War. This was an important step before reconstituting national defense planning on a "long-haul" basis.[33] The Administration inherited a $72.9 billion budget which President Truman had submitted to Congress on 9 January 1953. This included a $41.3 billion appropriation for the Department of Defense. This budget, reflecting the buildup which had taken place during Korea, was projected to create a deficit of $9.9 billion for FY 1954. More alarming, the cumulative deficit for wartime orders which had not been delivered was estimated by Eisenhower's budget director Joseph Dodge to reach approximately $56 billion by mid-1957.[34]

Pressure to bring these deficits under control was to be a central concern of the new administration. The New Look sought to bring about realistic expenditures on defense within the confines of a sound economy while placing primary reliance for deterring the Soviet threat on the nuclear retaliatory capabilities of the United States.

After the Korean War was brought to a close by the signing of the armistice on 27 July 1953, the Army was to find itself increasingly at odds with President Eisenhower's approach to national security. Eisenhower's New Look national security policy, when it was articulated, was to have profoundly unsettling implications for the United States Army. One aspect of this was a long-running battle between Eisenhower and General Matthew Ridgway. Ridgway had been appointed by Eisenhower as Chief of Staff of the Army in the summer of 1953. Previously Ridgway had been serving as NATOs Supreme Allied Commander, Europe (SACEUR) since May 1952. During his tenure as SACEUR, Ridgway pushed for NATO to realize its expansive 96 division force goal (which included both active and reserve divisions) approved at the February 1952 North Atlantic Council meeting in Lisbon.[35] Indeed, during Ridgway's tour as SACEUR, his headquarters completed a NATO force plan which attempted to assess the impact of atomic weapons on the European theater of operations that estimated even greater forces would be required to successfully defend Western Europe than had been projected in the Lisbon Force Goals.[36] This line of thinking was very much out-of-step with the New Look, and Ridgway's promotion to Chief of Staff allowed Eisenhower to move his old friend and former Chief of Staff General Alfred Gruenther to replace Ridgway as SACEUR.

Despite pressure for substantial fiscal reductions, President Eisenhower had characteristically initially sought a careful review of US policy options during the first half year of his presidency. This was undertaken through two separate appraisals. First, he initiated Project SOLARIUM, a study of US options for prosecuting the Cold War. Three task forces were formed to study possible policies for the prosecution of the Cold War. The studies were conducted at the National War College, facilitated by the Commandant, Lieutenant General H. A. Craig, US Air Force. Task Force–A advocated a continuance of the Truman administrations containment policy, Task Force–B stressed the importance of nuclear deterrence, and Task Force–C advocated a more aggressive "roll back" of Communism through the use of propaganda, covert operations, and maximum application of military power in pursuit of political aims. Though Eisenhower tried to stress common themes in the individual task forces, drafting a set of composite recommendations proved difficult. Nonetheless, Project SOLARIUM helped articulate the strategic choices available to the new administration.[37]

Parallel to this effort, Eisenhower appointed a fresh slate of Chiefs of Staff for each service (excepting Marine Corps Commandant General Lemuel Shepherd), including Ridgway, General Nathan Twining as Air Force Chief of Staff, Admiral Robert Carney as Chief of Naval Operations, and with Admiral Arthur Radford as Chairman of the JCS. Before they assumed office, Eisenhower instructed them to appraise the country's military capabilities then sequester themselves to develop a paper independent of any staff assistance that addressed the strategic concept, implementing plans, and roles and missions of the armed forces. They were also to review the composition and readiness of the forces, the implications of new weapons on military tactics, and the military assistance program.[38] The paper was presented to the NSC on 28 August 1953. It called for a considerable reduction in the size of US overseas deployments and the creation of a central reserve in the United States to respond to Cold War contingencies. Though ostensibly representing the agreement of the Chiefs of Staff, in the discussion which followed the fragility of the paper's consensus was soon exposed. Leading off, Chief of Naval Operations Carney pointed out that the papers' recommendations could only be understood in light of the effort to reconcile basic security considerations while meeting a budgetary limitation. Army Chief of Staff Ridgway was even more emphatic in stressing his reservations. Ridgway "desired to make it crystal clear that he did not subscribe to the withdrawal of our forces stationed overseas." He also pointed out that he did not believe that deterrence could be provided by a single military arm, implicitly criticizing over-reliance on the Air Force's Strategic Air Command.[39] Ridgway had been even more direct in his criticism of the "New Look" a few days earlier when addressing the Army Staff upon his arrival in Washington. In his address he stated, "It is not his [professional military] responsibility to decide whether the military means which he determines are the minimum essential to accomplish the military task assigned him will cost more than the Nation can afford."[40] With such an outlook, trouble was clearly brewing between Eisenhower's New Look and Ridgway's vision of the Army's role in defense.

Eisenhower was determined to achieve significant reductions in defense expenditure in order to put the national economy on a sounder basis. Further, he was convinced that the threat from the Soviet Union was best countered through deterrence premised on the massive retaliatory capability of the United States. This meant that strengthening the credibility of the nuclear deterrent was one of Eisenhower's primary goals. NSC 162/2, the initial Eisenhower era NSC statement of Basic National Security Policy, stated that "The major deterrent to aggression against Western Europe is the manifest determination of the United States to use its atomic capability and massive retaliatory striking power if the area is attacked."[41] In order to maintain a "strong military posture, with emphasis on the capability of inflicting massive retaliatory damage," NSC 162/2 called for the "maintenance of a sound, strong and growing economy, capable of providing . . . the strength . . . over the long pull."[42]

At a November meeting with Secretary of State Dulles, Secretary of the Treasury Humphrey, and Secretary of Defense Wilson, it was agreed that the emphasis on "new weapons," as nuclear weapons were euphemistically referred to, would justify a reduction in conventional forces, including ground troops and certain naval forces.[43] By December, the implication of this decision was spelled out for the services in JCS 2101/113, "Military Strategy and Posture." It projected a reduction in the Army budget from $13 billion to $10.2 billion and a reduction in manpower of just under 400,000 men. For Ridgway, there was more at stake than just the budgetary apportionment. A. J. Bacevich has argued that for Ridgway the New Look was a profound challenge to his conception of military professionalism because it seemed to imply that the "use of force had lost its value as an instrument of policy."[44]

During the remainder of his tenure as Chief of Staff, Ridgway directed resistance to Eisenhower's defense policy in a number of ways. Ridgway himself continued to oppose the New Look in the confines of the NSC and the JCS. Within the Army Staff, Ridgway found a close ally in Major General James Gavin, then the Assistant Chief of Staff for Operations (G-3). Gavin orchestrated a series of informal Saturday morning meetings of officers disaffected with the New Look to help refine the Army's critique of massive retaliation. When this approach had run its course to little effect late in 1954, Ridgway and other senior Army officers took their case to the public. Finally, the Army also refused to allow "massive retaliation" to fundamentally alter its approach to war.

Throughout the 1950s Army doctrine, training, and education continued to reflect the premise that force retained political utility and that destruction of an enemy's armed forces was the Army's primary goal in warfare.[45] In 1954 a revised edition of FM 100-5 was published. For Bacevich, one of the most important aspects of the 1954 edition lay in its use as a political document to advance Army Chief of Staff Matthew Ridgway's opposition to President Eisenhower defense policy.[46] In the introduction, the 1954 edition explicitly stated that "Indiscriminate destruction [of civilian populations] is unjustifiable in a military sense," and that, "The basic doctrine of Army operations is the defeat of an enemy by application of military power directly or indirectly against the armed forces which support his political structure."[47] The 1954 edition reaffirmed many of the principles laid down in the 1949 edition, but also included material which reflected the advent of the potential for a nuclear battlefield. A new section on Fire Support and Coordination in Chapter 8 on offensive operations was telling. This section stated explicitly that "Atomic weapons are an extremely powerful means of fire support."[48] Nonetheless, the integration of atomic weapons for fire support "Does not change tactical doctrine for the employment of firepower . . . planning and execution of offensive operations will continue to be based on the integration of fire and maneuver."[49] Thus, FM 100-5 stated that during peacetime the mission of the Army was to prepare itself to incapacitate the enemy's military capacity "By organization, training, equipment, and indoctrination of field units capable of performing their wartime mission." It was not revised again during the Eisenhower administration.[50] The Army remained wedded to preparing itself for its traditional role, unshaken by the tenets of the New Look which suggested a form of future war in which land combat might have little or no role.

Shortly after the completion of FM 100-5, Ridgway requested a hearing before the NSC to air his dissent with the New Look yet again. Consistent with the language of the recently published doctrine manual, Ridgway urged the NSC to consider abandoning massive retaliation and instead adopt a strategy "Based on the requirements of fighting rather than simply deterring a war."[51] The NSC rejected Ridgway's position. Eisenhower held a meeting with Secretary of Defense Wilson and the Joint Chiefs on 22 December 1954 to reiterate his commitment to massive retaliation as the centerpiece of his administration's national security policy.[52]

Frustrated by his inability to budge the NSC or the President, Ridgway took his criticism public in early 1955. In a series of addresses Ridgway stressed the need for an Army to defeat an opponent's armed forces in any future conflict. His attacks on the wisdom of massive retaliation as a deterrent strategy became increasingly vociferous. Major General Gavin participated in a Council on Foreign Relations study group on "Nuclear Weapons and Foreign Policy" where he stressed the importance of a conventional capability to counter the Red Army's potential to overrun Europe. The connection to the Council on Foreign Relations was an important window

20

to the Democratic foreign policy elite, and would prove to be an important forum for thinking about limited war and flexible response, but that lay in the future. Surprisingly, during the January and February Congressional hearings on the defense budget, Ridgway proved more muted and ambiguous on cuts to the Army than some had expected.[53]

By the spring of 1955, Ridgway's conflict with the administration was acute. With his two year term as Chief of Staff set to expire, it was deemed that Ridgway, having passed the mandatory age of 60, would be retired at the end of his term. Ridgway later argued strenuously in his memoirs that he and his wife had already made the personal decision to retire months before the official announcement was made.[54] But Ridgway's actions regarding and disposition toward the New Look made it inconceivable that Eisenhower would consider reappointing him. Thus on 30 June 1955 General Matthew Ridgway retired as Army Chief of Staff. He was replaced by General Maxwell Taylor, another member of the so-called "Parachute Club," who would serve as Army Chief of Staff until his (first) retirement in 1959.[55]

Amidst the ferment of Ridgway's tenure as Chief of Staff, a number of proposals for Army reorganization were also discussed.[56] On the Army-wide level, the most important of these had to do with the organization of the command of troops inside the continental United States. Continental Army Command (CONARC) was formed by re-designating the Office, Chief of Army Field Forces (AFF) as Headquarters, CONARC. CONARC was activated on 1 February 1955. In addition to the previous functions of AFF, CONARC assumed duties "of the Assistant Chief of Staff, G-3 for approving tables of organization and equipment and for preparing and reviewing tables of allowances." Initial organizational reforms did not improve CONARC's control over units in the CONUS sufficiently, so in April 1957 CONARC was given the authority of an overseas theater command. This increased CONARC's responsibilities over zone of the interior armies to include broad manpower, administrative, and logistical matters.[57] As a result of recommendations made in the "Report of the Officer Education and Training Review Board" in 1958, the Commanding General of CONARC was also designated Director of the Army School System in September 1960.[58] James Hewes argues that the "Establishment of CONARC as a unified field command represented a return to the wartime concept of Army Ground Forces."[59] CONARC would retain its essential features down to its dissolution in the STEADFAST reorganization of 1973. Some modifications did occur in 1962 which had implications for—among other things—the development of training, doctrine, and tables of organization and equipment.[60]

A new scheme was implemented on 3 January 1956 which included an expanded Army civilian secretariat, an expanded office of the Chief of Staff, and considerable reorganization of the staff components.[61] Within the office of Chief of Staff, two new agencies were formed, a Coordinating Group, and a Programs and Analysis Group. While the Coordination Group's formal mission was long-range strategic planning, in practice it served as an adjunct to Chief of Staff Taylor's goal of "spelling out the role of the Army in the national defense establishment."[62] The Coordination Group might thus be seen as a formalization of Gavin's Saturday morning bull sessions from the Ridgway era. It was not long before this new staff became involved in the so-called "revolt of the colonels."[63] The changing of the Chief of Staff did little to mute the Army's resistance to the New Look, rather it led the Army to pursue its institutional goals through new tactics.

The matter of the use of nuclear weapons by the armed forces was of course more than a philosophical debate between the Commander-in-Chief and his senior military advisers. If in fact nuclear weapons were to be used on the battlefield without question, then preparing the Army for atomic warfare became a matter of some importance. It would also present the Army with the problem of equipping and training for a "dual-capable" mission, as the progress of advances in technology suggested a divergence in the needs of a force that prepared for conventional war versus nuclear war. In mid-March 1955, both Secretary of State Dulles and President Eisenhower made public statements which suggested that the battlefield use of tactical nuclear weapons was becoming more likely. Dulles informed a news conference on 15 March that as smaller atomic munitions became available, it would decrease the likelihood of using city-destroying weapons.[64] The following day, President Eisenhower was asked to amplify on Dulles' statement of the previous day. In this news conference, he suggested that "In combat where these things [nuclear fission weapons] can be used on strictly military targets and for strictly military purposes, I see no reason why they shouldn't be used just exactly as you would use a bullet or anything else."[65] The situation, however, was not as clear as it might seem. For instance, SACEUR General Gruenther, while speaking with reporters at SHAPE in Paris on 15 March, had indicated that NATO only had plans to use nuclear weapons in the case of all-out war with the Soviets. The Chicago Daily Tribune reported this under the headline "Atomic Bombs Ruled Out for Small Wars."[66] General Gruenther, no doubt reflecting an outlook he closely shared with President

22

Eisenhower, might have easily explained this away by saying he did not believe in anything besides all-out war with the Soviets, but others in the Army establishment were more willing to press the issue.

During an initial meeting after General Taylor had become Chief of Staff, Eisenhower stressed to him the importance of teamwork with his fellow chiefs. Eisenhower also used the opportunity to revisit the question of the appropriate size for the Army's divisions. The President indicated to Taylor his preference for divisions of "small size with a pooling of tanks, AA, and other elements of this type." General Taylor responded that "after consideration and discussion of the problem, [it might be necessary] to take action by arbitrary decision" on the matter.[67] Eisenhower does not seem to have been unduly disturbed by Taylor's suggestion. The following year, when the size of US force levels in Europe again became an issue, Eisenhower consistently spoke in favor of "units reduced in size and overhead but with equivalent strength through increased fire-power as a result of tactical atomic weapons."[68]

When Taylor became Chief of Staff, the Joint Strategic Planning Committee was just getting underway with its annual planning cycle. Since 1952, the Joint Chiefs of Staff had stipulated that studies for long-range, mid-range, and short-range plans should be prepared on an annual cycle. These were the Joint Long-Range Strategic Estimate (JLRSE), the Joint Strategic Objective Plan (JSOP), and the Joint Strategic Capabilities Plan (JSCP). Ideally the first two were reviewed and approved each June, while the latter was reviewed in November and approved by 31 December. The preparation of the JSCP in late 1954 ran several months behind schedule due to the intra-service controversy over strategy and the conception of a required mobilization base. During the discussion of a Joint Medium Range War Plan (JMRWP) in late 1954-early 1955, the Air Force argued that after a short, intense nuclear bombing campaign, there was little likelihood of extended conventional hostilities along the lines of World War II. The Army-Navy-Marine Corps all argued for a more traditional conception, which called for the build-up of extensive force, and hence a large mobilization base, to prosecute the war after an initial nuclear exchange.[69]

In July 1955 the Joint Strategic Plans Committee began work on the Joint Strategic Capabilities Plan for 1956-57, followed by initial preparation of JSOP-60 the next month. During the preparation of these reports, the Army planning deputy achieved a concession from his Air Force colleague that allowed the insertion of language much more in line with the Army's views. The insertions contained the suggestion that general war might arise out of a series of actions and counter-actions by the Soviet Union and the United States that neither side had intended to lead to general war. In this event, both sides might seek to avoid or at least postpone the use of atomic weapons. While recognizing that this condition would probably not last long, its inclusion in the JSPC report to the JCS seemed to portent a shift towards a view more conducive to Army thinking.[70] This paper, however, soon drew the ire of Chairman of the Joint Chiefs Radford. In a memorandum of 28 March, he flatly stated that the suggestion that in general war the United States would not use atomic weapons from the outset represented a "radical departure from the present approved policy." He instructed the Chiefs and their planners to be clear that presently approved policy countenanced the immediate use of atomic weapons in general war and their utilization in local wars if the situation dictated, and that planning was to proceed with this guidance.[71] This policy proved insufficient to calm dissent from the Army's ranks. On 2 April, Chairman Radford and the Chiefs met with President Eisenhower, who reiterated that he was clear that in "any war with the Soviets we would use" atomic weapons. He also stressed his desire to see the long-term military budget "level-off" around $36.5 billion.[72]

Still Taylor could not be quelled. He was granted another session with the President, this time accompanied only by Chairman Radford, to state his case on 24 May. Returning to the theme which had driven Army comments on the JSCP, Taylor stressed the view that with the projected arrival of mutual deterrence around 1960, conceivably "any war that occurred would seem more likely to be a small war." President Eisenhower responded by returning to his well established position that in any war with the Soviets "Prudence would demand that we get our striking forces into the air immediately upon notice of hostile action," and though massive retaliation had been scoffed at, it was "Likely to be the key to survival." Eisenhower also stressed that he had no intention of tying down large scale forces in small wars on the Soviet periphery, hence, no more Koreas. At most he foresaw the deployment of a few Army battalions sent to critical spots to bolster indigenous forces. In the meantime, he wanted Taylor to focus on the incorporation of rockets and missiles into the Army ground forces, "with small mobile combat groups integrating their operations closely with them." General Taylor responded to all this by replying that it would "initiate fundamental and rather drastic changes [to the Army]." Eisenhower hoped that any such changes could be applied gradually, and would not necessarily be seen as radical. He concluded by stressing his time-worn admonition that the Chiefs rise above the narrow views of their services and focus on the development of a truly corporate view. To this end, they might consider constituting a group of retired senior officers and scientists who could address themselves to long-term thinking about defense planning bereft of administrative responsibilities.[73]

General Taylor was ready to propose a new tactical organization of the Army's divisions by fall 1956 that aimed at creating the "dual-capable" force which could fight both tactical nuclear engagements and conventional war. The organizational format presented in the fall 1956 had been worked up by Deputy Chief of Staff for Military Operations General Clyde Eddleman on Taylor's instructions. Officially known as Reorganization of the Current Infantry Division (ROCID), Reorganization of the Airborne Division (ROTAD), and Reorganization of the Current Armored Division (ROCAD), the project became known as the Pentomic division.[74]

This new organization had a number of antecedents. US airborne divisions in World War II had frequently operated as division task forces with extra regiments assigned.[75] As shown in the foregoing discussion, President Eisenhower himself had repeatedly and consistently stressed his own interest in smaller divisions.[76] Colonels Reinhardt and Kintner wrote in 1953 that they foresaw a need to do away with the inflexible regiment, and stress battalions that were "capable of a reasonable degree of self-sufficiency, logistically as well as tactically."[77] Then Chief of Staff Ridgway had authorized the development of an Atomic Field Army (AFTA-1) back in 1954. This design had been field tested on the 47th Infantry Division and 1st Armored Division in February 1955, and again during Exercise SAGEBRUSH. The latter was a large scale exercise conducted at Fort Polk, Louisiana in November and December 1955 which made use of extensive simulated tactical nuclear weapons. Dissatisfaction with this field test led the AFTA-1 concept to be officially abandoned in April 1956.[78] General James Gavin, Chief of Research and Development under Taylor, had conducted map exercises while head of US VII Corps in 1953-54 that suggested to him a need for "amorphous" infantry divisions repackaged into "small, widely dispersed battle groups," capable of operating in depths of over 100 miles. For Gavin it was clear that such divisions would have to have greatly increased air mobility and accurate, long-range missiles capable of delivering nuclear warheads.[79] Taylor had also experimented with a new divisional organization in South Korea in 1954. There he decided that improvements in communications would allow a divisional commander to direct up to five subordinate units.[80]

By late 1956, General Taylor was ready to implement a divisional reorganization for an interim period of five-years, subject to ongoing evaluation.[81] Taylor briefed the President on the new divisional structure on 11 October, and then he and General Eddleman articulated them for a wider audience at the Association of the United States Army's second annual meeting later in the month. The new divisions were to be based on five battle groups with organic atomic capability (originally in the form of an Honest John battery) which superseded and replaced the older triangular division with its three regiments.[82] This Pentomic structure would be reflected in each echelon of command. All the Pentomic divisions were also smaller than their predecessors, though this was less marked in the airborne divisions which had already been smaller than their infantry counterparts. The Pentomic infantry divisions were reduced from 17,000 to 13,700 men, and the airborne divisions to 11,500 men.[83] In order to increase the mobility of these divisions, it was also decided to cut back on tanks, armored personnel carriers, and artillery heavier than the 105mm gun. To compensate, they were equipped with additional unarmored anti-tank guns, including the 90mm and 106mm guns. The organic aviation of the Pentomic division was increased from 10 to 37 helicopters, but formidable logistic challenges persisted which were not fully addressed.[84] The 101st Airborne division was the first division reorganized along these lines to test the concept.[85] Eventually Taylor planned to convert all the airborne and infantry divisions to the Pentomic concept, on the five-year basis. The Army's armored divisions, however, were never reorganized along these lines.[86]

The first US Army to reorganize for fighting warfare in the atomic age was the 7th Army in Europe. Under the command of LTG Bruce Clarke, who had served in Patton's 3d Army in WWII, the 7th Army attempted to put the organizational priorities of the Pentomic era into practice. Clarke envisioned his field army, made up of six divisions, with four in contact, one in reserve, and one holding rear areas. Not surprisingly, this approximated the US forces then stationed in Germany. This field army was to be prepared to cover an area 100 miles wide and 200 miles deep with approximately 200,000 men. This considerable depth reflected one essential feature of the Pentomic army, its emphasis on dispersal of forces in order to make them less vulnerable to atomic attack. This emphasis on dispersal to receive an attack masked an underlying preference for the offensive. While NATO strategy was ostensibly defensive, Clarke issued a training directive that emphasized the offensive potential of an atomic equipped Army. It stated, "The attack is the key to success; the defense is merely a temporary expedient to converge forces for an attack elsewhere or to prepare for an attack at a future date." The training directive also stressed that, "The end sought in planning and executing an attack is brought about

26

by *deliberate planning and violent execution* [emphasis in original]. The opposite is fatal. *Speed* in planning is often needed, but *haste* should be avoided. Remember that in combat there is no second opportunity for rehearsals."[87] Clarke's emphasis on offense befitted the tactics embraced for Pentomic divisions, which emphasized the use of atomic fires to blast holes through enemy defenses, and then exploit the mobility of the battle groups to press through the holes opened by the battlefield atomic weapons.[88] One study of the Pentomic era suggested that far from a revolutionary doctrine, it instead harkened back to the conception of massed artillery fire employed by the French and British generals on the Western Front in World War I.[89]

By 1958, curricular changes were underway at the Army Command and General Staff College which reflected the attention being given to the nuclear battlefield. In an address to the CGSC graduating class of 1957, General Taylor informed them that "The Army is burning its military textbooks to clear away the old and make way for the new."[90] In 1957-58, the curriculum at Leavenworth was completely rewritten. After this exercise, students were spending 387 hours on tactical nuclear warfare, and by 1960 this had risen to 600 hours devoted to problems of general and tactical nuclear warfare.[91] The interest in the nuclear battlefield was also reflected in the pages of the Army's professional journals. There were 132 articles on nuclear combat published in *Military Review* in the years 1955 to 1959, versus 32 in the proceeding five years and 37 in the following five years.[92]

One other feature the shift to the Pentomic division was the increasing emphasis within the Army's research and development budget on missile technology. The Army had been an early and successful player in the development of the US missile arsenal, but by late in the decade its development projects were drawing increasing concern from the Air Force, who felt that Army long-range guided missiles impinged on their strategic delivery mission. Under a 1954 Department of Defense policy, the Army was authorized to develop surface-to-air missiles with a range of 50 miles, and ground bombardment missiles for operation within the loosely defined "zone of combat operations." With the advent of the tactical nuclear battlefield greatly expanded "zone of combat operations," the Army developed a commensurate interest in missiles with considerably greater ranges.

By late 1955 the United States had embarked on the development of intercontinental ballistic missile (ICBM) and intermediate range ballistic missile (IRBM) programs as matters of high priority. While the Air Force was given supervision over the ICBM effort and IRBM development, the Army and Navy were assigned to develop a second IRBM which could be used on land or sea. The Army, building on the success of its Redstone program, established an Army Ballistic Missile Agency at the Redstone Arsenal in Huntsville, Alabama headed by MG John B. Medaris. Beating the Air Force to the punch, it successfully tested a Jupiter-C IRBM in late September 1956.[93] The Navy's interest in lighter weight, solid fueled missiles soon led them to break away from the Army development project and proceed with the Polaris project. This created a budgetary problem for the Army project. The Army's development effort suffered an even more damaging blow in late November 1957 when Secretary of Defense Wilson ruled that the Army—regardless of its success with the Jupiter—would not be able to deploy weapons with a range greater than 200 miles.[94] But with the earlier Corporal and Honest John missiles having ranges of 75 and 22 miles respectively, the Army was still in search of an effective, mobile weapon for the Pentomic battlefield. After Wilson's decision, attention turned to improving the Redstone rocket. With its 175 mile range and liquid fuel propellant, it had its limitations. However, the Army was confident that it could adopt the solid-fuel propellant that the Navy was developing for the Polaris. This would reduce the Redstone's weight, potentially extending its range up to 400-500 miles. In one of their rare victories of the Pentomic era, the Army benefited from Eisenhower's own intervention in favor of the Redstone extension. At a meeting in early August 1957, he gave his blessing to the development of an Army missile with a range of 500 miles, negating Wilson's earlier decision on the matter.[95] By FY 1957 the fiscal impact of the Army's commitment to tactical nuclear weapons and missiles was having a telling impact, consuming 43 percent of the research and development budget, compared to less than 15 percent for vehicles, artillery, and aviation combined.[96]

General Maxwell Taylor stepped down as Army Chief of Staff in July 1959. After four years of opposing the implications of Eisenhower's New Look policy, Taylor was not reappointed to stand another term as Army Chief of Staff, though he was still three years from mandatory retirement and eligible for reappointment. When he left office, he quickly vocalized his criticism of Eisenhower's defense policy and decried the failure to modernize the US Army.[97] Following in the footsteps of his fellow "Parachute Club" members Ridgway and Gavin, Taylor published his dissent in a book titled *The Uncertain Trumpet*, which famously popularized the concept of "flexible response" that was to gain considerable traction in the Kennedy administration.[98] Taylor's successor as Chief of Staff of the Army was General Lyman Lemnitzer.[99] Taylor's idea for the Pentomic division, which had won little support within the Army and done nothing to reverse the declining trend of the Army budget in the later years of the Eisenhower administration, was also soon abandoned.[100]

The Dual-Capability Conundrum

Like his predecessors, CSA Lemnitzer argued that the Army needed to maintain a "dual capability," stress mobility, and focus on improved communications to deal with the potential ranges of the "modern" battlefield. It was important that this "dual capability" include sufficient non-nuclear potential that the Army "did not feel compelled to use nuclear weapons as the only alternative to failure." Because of advances in technology and equipment, Lemnitzer also wanted to make sure the Army's doctrine and tactical organizations were kept fully up to date, with doctrine being constantly re-examined.[101]

As early as January 1959, General Bruce Clarke, who had taken command of CONARC, had established a new study titled "Modern Mobile Army 1965-1970" (MOMAR I) to look at a successor to the ill-fated Pentomic division. Clarke had previously served as Commander of the US 7th Army during its attempted conversion to the Pentomic model. The MOMAR I design retained some of the features of the earlier Pentomic reorganization, but the divisions earlier battle groups were now replaced by "five self-sustained combat commands" which were a "hybrid of the regiments and combat commands of World War II." The MOMAR I concept also placed considerable emphasis on mechanized forces, with all units mounted in organic mechanized vehicles.[102] Thus, the MOMAR I concept adapted superficial features of the Pentomic division structure, while advancing a more clearly armor—versus airborne—influenced approach. Since Clarke himself was an old armored commander, this approach should come as no surprise. Despite widespread vetting of MOMAR I—including review at the Command and General Staff College and by a General Officers Board—it found little support amongst the Army Staff.[103]

It seems that the notion of dual-capability (or versatility, or flexibility) was causing considerable difficulty for the Army in settling on a new division format.[104] Vice Chief of Staff Eddleman, who also had previously served as both Commander, US 7th Army and Commander, United States Army Europe, wrote to CONARC Command in December 1960 that, "While MOMAR is useful as a reference, it does not provide the simplicity, homogeneity, versatility, and flexibility required by the Army for its diverse worldwide tasks in the coming decade."[105] Insofar as the MOMAR

I concept, with its emphasis on mechanization, seemed well-suited for a World War II-style conflict in northwest Europe, there is something to Eddleman's criticism. Yet at the same time, the Army had just rejected the lighter, more mobile Pentomic division, which might have turned out to be well-suited for deployments in areas where the US Army would not face opposition equipped with heavy armor.

Nonetheless, Eddleman and the Department of the Army's unhappiness with MOMAR led him to initiate yet another study of the division. Prior to Eddleman's criticism, a study group at the Command and General Staff College which had been reviewing the MOMAR concept during 1960 had already suggested the possibility of a division that could be tailored to fit operational conditions based on a building-block model. Eddleman instructed CONARC to develop a design plan for a type of division with a manpower ceiling of 15,000 that would be as similar as possible to other divisions.[106] This new study was titled the Reorganization Objective Army Division (ROAD 65).

The Kennedy Administration

Senator John F. Kennedy narrowly defeated Eisenhower's Vice President, Richard Nixon, in the presidential elections of November 1960. The Kennedy campaign platform, making use of the general unhappiness with massive retaliation in the United States and amongst its allies, instead adopting a defense posture known as "flexible response."[107] This signaled the end to what General Maxwell Taylor called the Army's "Babylonian captivity." Indeed, after Kennedy's own frustration over military advice during the Bay of Pigs fiasco, he called the flamboyant Taylor out of retirement and installed him in the White House as the special military advisor to the President. Later, once General Lyman Lemnitzer was sent to Paris to replace SACEUR Lauris Norstad, a perceived devotee of Eisenhower's New Look, Taylor was installed as Chairman of the Joint Chiefs of Staff (1962-64), and later served as US Ambassador to Vietnam during the steady expansion of US involvement there.

Once in office, the Kennedy administration quickly worked to demonstrate its resolve to improve the perceived failings of Eisenhower's defense program.[108] President John F. Kennedy, delivered a Special Message to Congress on Urgent National Needs on 25 May 1961. In this address he stated that Secretary of Defense McNamara had been instructed to reorganize and modernize the Army's divisional structure. The object of this latest reorganization aimed to "increase [the divisions] non-nuclear

30

firepower, to improve its tactical mobility in any environment, to insure its flexibility to meet any direct or indirect threat, to facilitate its coordination with our major allies, and to provide more modern mechanized divisions in Europe and bring their equipment up to date."[109] This was done along the lines of the ROAD division, which had been approved by Army Chief of Staff General George Decker on 14 April 1961.[110] The Cold War crisis over Berlin, which had entered another tense phase after the Kennedy–Khrushchev summit in Vienna in the summer of 1961, delayed the initial reorganization along ROAD lines until the following year. Interestingly, the ROAD concept was implemented without conducting any field tests.[111] The reorganization of the Army's divisions into ROAD was complete by 1964. These new divisions had three brigade headquarters with no fixed maneuver units assigned. The flexibility of the ROAD structure was rooted in the ability to assign from two to five battalions of varying types given the situation. The composition of the mix would then determine the division type.[112] As a practical matter, however, the divisions battalion complements became relatively fixed since the Army had insufficient resources to maintain an independent pool of non-divisional maneuver battalions for later assignment.[113]

During the initial enthusiasm for "flexible response," the Army's budget appropriations grew; ROAD became the post-Pentomic divisional structure; a new edition of FM 100-5 was produced in 1962; and Special Forces and counterinsurgency received a great deal of emphasis.[114] Renewed emphasis on conventional warfare was reflected in the school curriculum. At Leavenworth, the number of class hours devoted to the nuclear battlefield, which had reached a high of 600 hours in the late 1950s, was reduced to 53 hours in 1961, and further trimmed to 16 hours by 1966. Conversely, instruction in counterinsurgency increased from 35 hours to 222 hours between 1961 and 1969.[115] While the ROAD concept predominated throughout the Vietnam era, the Army continued experimentation with increased mobility for its divisions. The establishment of the 1st Cavalry Division as an airmobile division based on a study by the Howze Board is typically touted as the leading example of experimentation in the early 1960s.[116]

Summary

Determining the role of the Army in the seeming heyday of nuclear warfare proved to be the major conceptual challenge for US Army leaders in the 1950s. Commandant Manton Eddy of the Command and General Staff College was an early visionary in this regard. Though there were never fully satisfactory answers to what the atomic battlefield would look like, Eddy ensured that students at CGSC were at the forefront of grappling with this problem. While exercises such as the DESERT ROCK series of tests in Nevada and SAGEBRUSH in Louisiana had considerable limitations, they represented legitimate attempts by the Army to explore a potential combat environment that was tremendously difficult to deal with in any more realistic way. These represented legitimate attempts, within the technological constraints of the day, to deal with the dilemmas of warfare in the atomic age.

Subsequent criticism aimed at the Army's conduct during the Pentomic era often fails to highlight this dilemma in the 1950s of realistically simulating the nature of future warfare. The essential feature of the era is that despite the tensions between Eisenhower and his Army Chiefs of Staff, the Army's attempt to deal with the challenges presented by the nuclear age were consonant with the national security strategy articulated by the Eisenhower administration. President Eisenhower repeatedly pointed out that he did not intend to use military force to fight limited wars on the Asian littoral, and that he found it inconceivable that there could be any form of limited war with the Soviets in Europe (or anywhere else). In the rare instances where Eisenhower did employ US military forces abroad, it was for brief shows of force, such as the deployment to Lebanon in 1958.[117] When this is taken together with his repeated preference for a smaller divisional structure and the Army's own search for a divisional structure adapted to atomic age warfare, it is hardly surprising that the Pentomic division emerged.[118] The switch to "flexible response" under the Kennedy administration, the attendant reorganization of Army divisions along the ROAD model, and increased spending on conventional (or general purpose forces, as they were referred to) served to allay tensions between the executive and the Army in the short term.[119] However, the shift in national strategy to "flexible response" did not prove a cure all for civil-military relations nor did it necessarily produce significant improvements (the Howze Board excepted) in Army learning and adaptation in the course of the 1960s.

32

Notes

1. A. C. Bacevich, *The Pentomic Era: The US Army Between Korea and Vietnam* (Washington, DC: National Defense University Press, 1986), pp.134-40; and Weigley, *History of the United States Army*, enlarged edition, pp.537-38. The Pentomic reorganization is treated more sympathetically in Wilson, *Maneuver and Firepower*, pp.270-86; and Ingo W. Trauschweizer, "Creating Deterrence for Limited War: The U.S. Army and the Defense of West Germany, 1953-1982" (PhD Dissertation, University of Maryland, 2006), especially p.213. Available at: https://drum.umd.edu/dspace/bitstream/1903/3390/1/umi-umd-3202.pdf. Trauschweizer's monograph will be published with the University of Kansas Press in the summer of 2008 as *The Cold War U.S. Army*. A dissertation by Paul C. Jussel, "Intimidating the World: The United States Atomic Army, 1956-1960" (PhD Dissertation: Ohio State University, 2004), brought to this author's attention in the late editing stages of this project, also provides a close analysis of the period. Available at: http://www.ohiolink.edu/etd/send-pdf.cgi/Jussel%20Paul%20C.pdf?acc_num=osu1085083063.

2. Bacevich's *The Pentomic Era: The US Army Between Korea and Vietnam* has been the standard history of the US Army in this era, though the publication of Trauscheizer's *The Cold War U.S. Army* will provide a valuable addition to our understanding of the period. For a succinct description of the Pentomic division, one should consult Glen R. Hawkins and James Jay Carafano, *Prelude to Army XXI: U.S. Army Division Design Initiatives and Experiments 1917-1995* (Washington, DC: Center of Military History, 1997), pp.13-14, and Wilson, *Maneuver and Firepower*, pp.270-86.

3. See David Alan Rosenberg's seminal article on the development of US nuclear war planning, "The Origins of Overkill: Nuclear Weapons and American Strategy, 1945-1960," *International Security*, v.7, n.4 (Spring 1983), pp.3-71. Also Walter S. Poole, *History of the Joint Chiefs of Staff, The Joint Chiefs of Staff and National Policy, v.IV: 1950-1952* (Washington, DC: Office of Joint History, 1998), pp.75-92 [hereafter HJCS]. For two excellent studies of the general strategic issues of the nuclear age, see Lawrence Freedman, *The Evolution of Nuclear Strategy*, 2nd edn. (New York: St. Martin's Press, 1989), and Scott D. Sagan, *Moving Targets: Nuclear Strategy and National Security* (Princeton: Princeton University Press, 1989).

4. Boyd L. Dastrup, *The US Army Command and General Staff College: A Centennial History* (Manhattan, KS: Sunflower University Press, 1982), p.90.

5. Harry P. Ball, *Of Responsible Command: A History of the U.S. Army War College*, revised edition. (Carlisle Barracks, PA: The Alumni Association of the United States Army War College, 1994) , pp.257, 282-83.

6. On the Naval War College, see John B. Hattendorf, *Sailors and Scholars: The Centennial History of the United States Naval War College* (Newport, RI:

Naval War College Press, 1984). This author is unaware of a comparable history of the Air War College.

7. Dastrup, *The US Army Command and General Staff College*, p.93.

8. Ibid.

9. G. C. Reinhardt and W. R. Kintner, *Atomic Weapons in Land Combat* (Harrisburg, PA: The Military Service Publishing Co., 1953).

10. Dastrup, *The US Army Command and General Staff College*, pp.101-02.

11. Ball, *Of Responsible Command*, rev. edn.. pp.284-89, 305-11. The war game played at the end of the 1952-53 session is telling, in that it was "designed to test student war plans for the first *six months* [emphasis added] of a war in Europe," see p.307. Even six months of combat in Western Europe by early 1953 could only be imagined if one took little account of SACs planned atomic bombardment of the Soviet Union, and instead looked at future war in Europe through the lens of past experience.

12. Charles Shrader has written that, "Beginning in 1949, ORO [US Army's Operations Research Office] conducted a number of groundbreaking in-depth studies of nuclear warfare," though it is not clear when the first of these studies were available to consumers. Charles R. Shrader, *History of Operations Research in the United States Army*, vol.I: *1942-1962* (Washington, DC: Office of the Deputy Under Secretary of the Army for Operations Research, United States Army, 2006), p.100. The literature discussing atomic battlefields in the 1950s is considerable. For a good overview, see Charles E. Heller and Elizabeth R. Snoke, *CSI Historical Bibliography No.1: The Integrated Battlefield 1945-1965* (Fort Leavenworth, KS: Combat Studies Institute, July 1980), available at: http://www.cgsc.army.mil/carl/resources/csi/heller2/heller2.asp.

13. Condit, *HOSD*, v.II: *The Test of War 1950-1953*, pp.469-70.

14. For the best account of Project VISTA, see David C. Elliot, "Project Vista and Nuclear Weapons in Europe," *International Security*, v.11, n.1 (Summer 1986), pp.163-83. James Gavin later served as Army Assistant Chief of Staff for Operations, G-3, and Chief of Research and Development. He participated in Project VISTA as a member of the Weapons System Evaluation Group. See James M. Gavin, *War and Peace in the Space Age* (New York: Harper & Brothers, 1958), pp.129-35.

15. Elliot, "Project Vista and Nuclear Weapons in Europe," p.176.

16. For the first review of conclusions by the VISTA group, see VISTA, Notes taken by Garrison Norton, 12 November 1951, DDRS, 1997, F51, 661. There is also a copy in Dwight D. Eisenhower Library [hereafter DDEL], Norstad Papers, Box 41. For the February version, see Epitome of the Summary of the Final Report of Project Vista, 12 February 1952, DDRS 1996, F45, 584. Some of the results of the VISTA story were leaked, and appeared in an article by Hanson Baldwin, "Experts Urge Tactical Air Might; Score Stress on Big Atom Bomber," *New York Times*, 5 June 1952, p.13.

17. Elliot, "Project Vista and Nuclear Weapons in Europe," p.177.

18. Epitome of the Summary of the Final Report of Project Vista, 12 February 1952, DDRS, 1996, F45, 584.

19. The exercise was publicly known as DESERT ROCK after Camp Desert Rock, but the nuclear tests were conducted under the codename BUSTER-JANGLE. The bomb dropped on 1 November (BUSTER) was a 20-kiloton weapon. However, two 1.2 kiloton weapons (JANGLE) were detonated later in November. For more on the BUSTER-JANGLE test series, see *Defense's Nuclear Agency 1947-1997* (Washington, DC: Defense Threat Reduction Agency, 2002), pp.80-86. Also, Gladwin Hill, "4 of Atom Unit Hail the Tactical Bomb," *New York Times*, 3 November 1951, p.6, and "Troops Endure Giant A-Bomb in Desert Test," *Chicago Daily Tribune*, 2 November 1951, p.11.

20. "The Atomic Background," *Armor*, v.LXI, n.4 (July-August 1952), p.12.

21. *Defense's Nuclear Agency 1947-1997*, p.86.

22. "Pace Hails Army's Atomic Gun, Cites U.S. Power in New Weapons," *New York Times*, 9 May 1952, p.1. The address was reprinted in *Armor*, v.LVI, n.3 (May-June 1952), pp.40-41.

23. On guided missile developments, see Condit, *HOSD*, v.II: *The Test of War 1950-1953*, pp.473-75. Only twenty 280mm cannons were ever made. They were capable of firing the W-9, and later W-19, nuclear artillery shells, with a 15-kiloton yield. They were retired from service in 1963. See Thomas D. Cochran, et. al. *Nuclear Weapons Databook*, vol.I: *U.S. Nuclear Forces and Capabilities* (Cambridge, MA: Ballinger Publishing, 1984), pp.7-10.

24. DDEL, White House Office, Office for Special Assistant for National Security Affairs [hereafter WHO, OSA for NSA], NSC Series, Statues of Projects Subseries, Box 5, NSC 5509, Pt. 1: Department of Defense Report to National Security Council on Status of United States Military Programs as of 31 December 1954. There is also a copy in DDRS, 2001, F189, 2458.

25. DDEL, WHO, OSA for NSA, NSC Series, Status of Projects Subseries, Box 3, NSC 161, 30 June 1953. There is also a copy in DDRS, 1990, F11, 165.

26. Doughty, *The Evolution of US Army Tactical Doctrine*, p.12.

27. Quoted in Dennis J. Vetock, *Lessons Learned: A History of US Army Lesson Learning* (Carlisle Barracks, PA: US Army Military History Institute, 1988), p.85.

28. FM 100-5 (Washington, DC: Department of the Army, 1954), p.6.

29. The presumption that the Soviets would quickly overrun Western Europe was a consistent feature of US war plans in the years after World War II. See Steven T. Ross, *American War Plans 1945-1950* (New York: Garland Publishing, 1988); and Stephen T. Ross and David Alan Rosenberg, eds. *America's Plans for War Against the Soviet Union 1945-1950*, 15 vols. (New York: Garland Publishing, 1989).

30. Doughty, *The Evolution of US Army Tactical Doctrine*, p.12. General Charles Bolte wrote in 1954 that the success of the Eighth Army "can be attributed in part to reliance on firepower rather than mere manpower." General Charles L. Bolte, "The Principal Address" *Armor*, v.LXIII, n.2 (March-April 1954), p.27.

31. Major General Robert W. Grow, "One Way to Lose a War!," *Armor*, v.LXII, n.1 (January-February 1953), pp.6-9.

32. "Address of General Jacob L. Devers," *Armor*, v.LXII, n.2 (March-April 1953), pp.20-21.

33. Stephen E. Ambrose, *Eisenhower*, vol.2: *The President* (New York: Simon and Schuster, 1984), p.34. On Eisenhower's conception of strategy during his presidency, see Robert R. Bowie and Richard H. Immerman, *Waging Peace: How Eisenhower Shaped an Enduring Cold War Strategy* (New York: Oxford University Press, 1998), esp. chap.8; Saki Dockrill, *Eisenhower's New-Look National Security Policy, 1953-1961* (Basingstoke, England: Macmillan Press, 1996); Andrew P. N. Erdmann, "War no longer has any logic whatever: Dwight D. Eisenhower and the thermonuclear revolution" in *Cold War Statesmen Confront the Bomb: Nuclear Diplomacy since 1945*, edited by John Lewis Gaddis, et. al. (Oxford: Oxford University Press, 1999); Steven Metz, "Eisenhower and the Planning of American Grand Strategy," *Journal of Strategic Studies*, v.14 (March 1991), pp.49-71; and Steven Metz, *Eisenhower as Strategist: The Coherent Use of Power in War and Peace* (Carlisle, PA: Strategic Studies Institute, US Army War College, 1993); and William B. Pickett, *Dwight David Eisenhower and American Power* (Wheeling, IL: Harlan Davidson, 1995).

34. Richard M. Leighton, *HOSD*, v.III: *Strategy, Money, and the New Look 1953-1956* (Washington, DC: Office of the Secretary of Defense, 2001), pp.65-67.

35. Condit, *HOSD*, v.II: *The Test of War 1950-1953*, pp.369-77; Walter S. Poole, *The History of the Joint Chiefs of Staff*, vol.IV: *1950-1952* (Wilmington, DE: Michael Glazier, 1980), p.293, and George C. Mitchell, *Matthew B. Ridgway: Soldier, Statesman, Scholar, Citizen* (Mechanicsburg, PA: Stackpole Books, 2002), pp.118-19.

36. DDEL, Norstad Papers, Box 41, SHAPE/411/53, 11 April 1953. The report stated, "it is unmistakably clear that, throughout the foreseeable future, conventional forces much greater than those that exist today will be required both to halt the enemy offensive and to initiate major counter-offensives to win the war."

37. For good accounts of the SOLARIUM exercise, see Dockrill, *Eisenhower's New-Look National Security Policy, 1953-1961*, pp.33-35, and Bowie and Immerman, *Waging Peace*, pp.123-43.

38. Stephen J. Jurika, Jr., ed., *From Pearl Harbor to Vietnam: The Memoirs of Arthur Radford* (Stanford, CA: Hoover Institute Press, 1980), pp.320-21.

39. DDEL, DDEP (Ann Whitman File), NSC Series, Box 4, Discussion at the 160th NSC Meeting, 27 August 1953.

40. This address to the Army Staff was printed in "The Army's New Chief of Staff," *Armor*, v.LXII, n.5 (September-October 1953), p.7. See also Matthew B. Ridgway, *Soldier: The Memoirs of Matthew B. Ridgway* (New York: Harper & Brothers, 1956), pp.269-73, 342-52, and A. J. Bacevich, "The Paradox of Professionalism: Eisenhower, Ridgway, and the Challenge to Civilian Control, 1953-1955," *The Journal of Military History*, v.61, n.2 (April 1997), p.312.

41. *FRUS 1952-1954*, v.II: *National Security Policy*, NSC 162/2, 30 October 1953, p.585.

42. Ibid., p.582.

43. *FRUS 1952-1954*, v.II: *National Security Policy*, Memorandum for Record by the President, 11 November 1953, p.597.

44. Bacevich, "The Paradox of Professionalism," pp.314-15.

45. Ibid., pp.317-18. There is also useful account of the problem of formulating doctrine in the Pentomic era in Kevin P. Sheehan, "Preparing for an Imaginary War?: Examining Peacetime Functions and Changes of Army Doctrine" (PhD dissertation, Harvard University, 1988), pp.97-141.

46. Bacevich, "The Paradox of Professionalism," pp.326-29.

47. FM 100-5 (1954 edition), p.5.

48. Ibid., p.94.

49. Ibid., p.96.

50. The next revision of FM 100-5 was published in 1962.

51. Bacevich, "The Paradox of Professionalism," p.321. This presentation was made at the 227th Meeting of the NSC on 3 December 1954.

52. This meeting was attended by Secretary of Defense Wilson, Undersecretary Anderson, and the four service chiefs with Colonel Goodpaster taking notes. President Eisenhower stated that, "As Commander-in-Chief he is entitled to the loyal support of his subordinates of the official position he has adopted, and he expects to have it." DDEL, White House Office, NSC Council Staff Papers, Disaster File, Box 4.

53. The official DOD historian of this period has written: "What might be called Ridgway's net position, based on all his testimony, turned out to be a mixture of ambiguity, uncertainty, and simple wait-and-see noncommitment." See Leighton, *HOSD*, v.III, pp.364-76.

54. Ridgway, *Soldier*, pp.259-60.

55. Ridgway, Taylor, and Gavin had all commanded airborne divisions in World War II. They were referred to under a number of nicknames, including the "Parachute Club," the "Airborne Club," and the "Airborne Mafia." For Taylor's own account of his time as Chief of Staff, see Maxwell D. Taylor, *Swords and Plowshares: A Memoir* (New York: De Capo Press, 1972), pp.164-77. He would be called out of retirement by President John F. Kennedy in 1961, first in the novel role of Special Military Adviser to the President, and later as Chairman of the Joint Chiefs of Staff.

56. Army reorganization plans are discussed in considerable detail in James E. Hewes, Jr., *From Root to McNamara: Army Organization and Administration 1900-1963* (Washington, DC: Center of Military History, 1975), pp.216-39.

57. Hewes, *From Root to McNamara*, p.268. The functions of the Army Staff after the April 1957 reorganization are spelled out in some detail in the October 1957 edition of *Armed Forces Management*.

58. The Army War College, however, was placed directly under the Department of the Army in June 1960. The Deputy Chief of Staff for Military Operations exercised supervisory responsibility. Ball, *On Responsible Command*, rev. edn., p.349.

59. Hewes, *From Root to McNamara*, p.269.

60. These were the result of a review (Project 80, better known as the Hoelscher Committee, as modified by the Traub Committee) initiated by then Secretary of Defense Robert McNamara. These reviews resulted in the elimination of five of the old technical service chiefs and their replacement by the Army Material Command and the Combat Development Command (CDC). CDC absorbed the responsibilities for developing Tables of Organization and Equipment as well as the preparation of field manuals. All of the technical bureaus training functions henceforth fell under CONARC. Hewes, *From Root to McNamara*, pp.316-364.

61. The reorganization was spelled out in Change 13 to Special Regulation 10-5-1 of 27 December 1955.

62. Hewes, *From Root to McNamara*, pp.239-41.

63. E. Bruce Geelhoed, *Charles E. Wilson and Controversy at the Pentagon, 1953-1957* (Detroit, MI: Wayne State University Press, 1979), pp.136-38. The controversy was partially sparked by the deliberate leak of an Army Staff paper critical of Air Force war plans. See "Excerpts From Army Staff Paper Asking Basic Change in Military Set-Up," Special to the *New York Times*, 24 June 1956, p.46.

64. "Dulles Says U.S. Pins Retaliation on Small A-Bomb," *New York Times*, 15 March 1955, p.1.

65. President's News Conference, 16 March 1955. *Public Papers of the President, 1955*, pp.330.

66. "Atomic Bombs Ruled Out For Small Wars," *Chicago Daily Tribune*, 16 March 1955, p.B7.

67. DDEL, DDEP, Ann Whitman File, Box 6, Memorandum of Conference with the President, 29 June 1955.

68. Quoted in note 4 to *FRUS 1955-1957*, v.IV, Doc.35, p.94. Eisenhower made this comment in a 12 August meeting with senior advisers on American force levels in Europe. The British had approached the Americans a month before about revising the NATO strategic concept with an aim to drawing down their own forces. Then on 13 July, the so-called "Radford Plan" calling for considerable reduction in US force levels by 1960 had been made public. With Mutual

Security legislation making its way through Congress and US allies in Europe expressing nervousness about the "Radford Plan," the Eisenhower administration was attempting to balance between Allied pressures and Eisenhower's New Look. For the British approach to the US for a new NATO strategy, see *FRUS 1955-57*, v. IV, Docs.32-34, pp.84-92. On the "Radford Plans" public airing, see "Military 'New Look' Badgers Pentagon," *Christian Science Monitor*, 13 July 1956, p.1 and "Radford Seeking 800,000-Man Cut; 3 Services Resist," *New York Times*, 13 July 1956, p.1. On West German concern over the "Radford Plan" and its implications for NATO, DDRS, 2000, F60, 765, Ltr., Konrad Adenauer to John Foster Dulles, 22 July 1956 (original in DDEL, Dulles Papers, General Correspondence & Memoranda Series, Box 2). This letter is reproduced in Hans-Peter Schwarz, *Konrad Adenauer*, vol.2: *The Statesman, 1952-1967*, trans. by Geoffrey Penny (Providence, RI: Berghahn Books, 1991), pp.234-5.

69. Kenneth W. Condit, *HJCS*, v.VI: *The Joint Chiefs of Staff and National Policy*, pp.31-2.

70. Ibid., pp.31-2, and Bacevich, *The Pentomic Era*, pp.46-47.

71. NARA, RG 218, Chairman's Files-Radford, Box 54, Memorandum: Strategic Concept and Use of US Military Forces, 28 March 1956.

72. DDEL, WHO, Office of the Staff Secretary, Subject Series, Defense Subseries, Box 4, Memorandum of Conference with the President, 2 April 1956.

73. DDEL, DDEP (Ann Whitman File), DDE Diary, Box 15, Memorandum of Conference, 24 May 1956.

74. DDEL, WHO, OSA for NSA, NSC Series, Status of Projects Subseries, Box 7, NSC 5720, Part 1, p.93; and Hawkins and Carafano, *Prelude to Army XXI*, pp.13-14.

75. McGrath, *The Brigade*, p.59.

76. I stress this point in particular to serve as a corrective to Kalev I. Sepp, "The Pentomic Puzzle: The Influence of Personality and Nuclear Weapons on U.S. Army Organization 1952-1958," *Army History* (Winter 2001), pp.1-13. Sepp has argued that, "Military orthodoxy and doctrinal logic called for armoring and mechanizing most U.S. Army combat divisions in response to the introduction of tactical nuclear weapons. The rejection of this approach, in the face of all the available evidence and examples, can only be attributed to the coincidental positioning of Generals Ridgway, Taylor, and Gavin in the key leadership posts of the U.S. Army at the time the nuclear revolution arrived on the battlefield."

77. Reinhardt and Kintner, *Atomic Weapons in Land Combat*, p.202.

78. Hawkins and Carafano, *Prelude to Army XXI*, pp.10-11. For more on Exercise Sagebrush, see "Exercise Sagebrush," *Armor*, v.LXV, n.1 (January-February 1956), pp.10-14, and John D. Stevenson, "Exercise Sagebrush: Massive Air-Ground Lesson in Atomic Warfare," *Air University Quarterly Review*, v.VIII, n.4 (Fall 1956), pp.15-38.

79. Gavin, *War and Peace in the Space Age*, pp.137-39.

80. John M. Taylor, *An American Soldier: The Wars of General Maxwell Taylor* (Novato, CA; Presidio Press, 1989), p.198. See Sepp, "The Pentomic Puzzle," p.10 for a critical view of Taylor's experiments in South Korea.

81. DDRS, 1982, F175, 2403, Appraisal of Capabilities of Conventional Forces, pt.V: Plan for Reorganization of Army Divisions, 12 May 1961.

82. Weigley, *History of the United States Army*, enlarged edition, p.537.

83. DDEL, WHO, OSA for NSA, NSC Series, Status of Projects Subseries, Box 7, NSC 5720, 30 June 1957. Also DDRS, 1982, F175, 2403, Appraisal of Capabilities of Conventional Forces, pt.V: Plan for Reorganization of Army Divisions, 12 May 1961.

84. Bacevich, *The Pentomic Era*, pp.106-08.

85. See Taylor and Eddleman's addresses to the Association of the United States Army, Second Annual Meeting, 25-27 October 1956 in *Army*, v.7, n.5 (December 1956), pp.20-30.

86. Sepp, "The Pentomic Puzzle," pp.10-11.

87. LTG Bruce C. Clarke, "Design for an Atomic Army," *Army*, v.8, n.6 (January 1958), pp.20-6. The phrase 'deliberate planning and violent execution' had been used by General Jacob Devers in his address to the 64th Annual Meeting of the United States Armor Association. See "Address of General Jacob L. Devers," *Armor*, v.LXII, n.2 (March-April 1954), p.21.

88. Theodore C. Mataxis and Seymour L. Goldberg, *Nuclear Tactics, Weapons, and Firepower in the Pentomic Division, Battle Group, and Company* (Harrisburg, PA: The Military Service Publishing Company, 1958), esp. pp.159-212 is typical of this line of thought.

89. Bacevich, *The Pentomic Era*, pp.108-09.

90. Ibid., p.53.

91. Dastrup, *The US Army Command and General Staff College*, pp.101-02.

92. Rose, *The Evolution of U.S. Army Nuclear Doctrine*, p.57.

93. Watson, *HOSD*, v.IV: *Into the Missile Age, 1956-1960*, pp.160-62.

94. Ibid., p.164.

95. Ibid., p.169.

96. Bacevich, *The Pentomic Era*, p.100.

97. Bem Price, "Why General Taylor is Unhappy Over Our Defense," *The Washington Post*, 5 July 1959, p.E1.

98. Maxwell D. Taylor, *The Uncertain Trumpet* (New York: Harper & Brothers, 1959).

99. Unlike his two immediate predecessors, Lemnitzer never published an autobiography. See James L. Binder, *Lemnitzer: A Soldier for His Time* (Washington, DC: Brassey's, 1997).

100. On the demise of the Pentomic concept, see Hawkins and James Jay Carafano, *Prelude to Army XXI: U.S. Army Division Design Initiatives and Experiments 1917-1995*, p.14.

101. General Lyman L. Lemnitzer, "Why We Need a Modern Army," *Army*, v.10, n.2 (September 1959), pp.16-21.

102. Hawkins and Carafano, *Prelude to Army XXI*, p.15.

103. Ibid.

104. See the exchange by Colonel Francis X. Bradley, Colonel Arthur S. Collins, and Colonel William E. DePuy in *Army*, October 1959, November 1959, and January 1960, respectively.

105. Quoted in Doughty, *The Evolution of US Army Tactical Doctrine*, p.20.

106. Hawkins and Carafano, *Prelude to Army XXI*, p.16.

107. In the campaign itself, the Kennedy team argued that the Eisenhower administrations complacent reaction to Sputnik and the Soviet ICBM program had created a missile gap. Eisenhower and Nixon knew this was not the case, but were unable to divulge why they remained confident of US missile superiority due to concern it would expose the extent of US aerial reconnaissance of the Soviet Union. The traditional account of "flexible response" is Jane E. Stromseth, *The Origins of Flexible Response: NATO's Debate Over Strategy in the 1960s* (Basingstoke, England: Macmillan Press, 1988). Also of value is Charles DeVallon Dugas Bolles, "The Search for an American Strategy: The Origins of the Kennedy Doctrine, 1936-1961" (PhD Dissertation, University of Wisconsin, 1985). For an alternative take on 'flexible response' which stresses its rhetorical, versus its operative, nature, see Francis J. Gavin, "The Myth of Flexible Response: United States Strategy in Europe during the 1960s," *The International History Review*, v.XXIII, n.4 (December 2001), pp.847-75. The Army's enthusiasm for flexible response would wane with deepening involvement in Vietnam. Thereafter flexible response became synonymous with "gradualism." The strong pejorative regard for "gradualism" was reflected as late as the Gulf War, when then Chairman of the Joint Chiefs of Staff Colin Powell would advance the so-called Powell Doctrine, which argued that US forces should only intervene overseas when there was a clear national security threat to US interests, there was clear public support for the intervention, and when overwhelming military forces could be brought to bear. For instance, Raymond J. Barrett, "Graduated Response and the Lessons of Vietnam," *Military Review*, v.LII, n.5 (May 1972), pp.80-91, future SACUER Wesley K. Clark, "Gradualism and American Military Strategy," *Military Review*, v.LV, n.9 (September 1975), pp.3-13, and John M. Collins, "Vietnam Postmortem: A Senseless Strategy," *Parameters*, v.VIII, n.1 (March 1978), pp.8-14.

108. The History of the Office of the Secretary of Defense now has a volume published which covers the Kennedy years. See Lawrence S. Kaplan, et.al., *History of the Office of the Secretary of Defense*, vol.V: *The McNamara Ascendancy 1961-1965* (Washington, DC: Office of the Secretary of Defense, 2006).

109. John F. Kennedy, Special Message to Congress on Urgent National Needs, 25 May 1961. Available at: http://www.presidency.ucsb.edu/ws/.

110. Hawkins and Carafano, *Prelude to Army XXI*, p.17, and Wilson, *Maneuver*

and Firepower, pp.293-314. General Maxwell Taylor, not surprisingly, was unenthusiastic about the ROAD concept. He wrote General Bruce Clark, Commander, US Army Europe in June 1961 that: "Personally, I have seen no evidence which indicates that there is a fundamental need for such a reorganization. It seems to me that the complaints about the lightness of the Pentomic Division could be overcome by appropriate attachments and reinforcements without a complete overhaul of structure." National Defense University, Digitial Collections (Online), Maxwell D. Taylor Papers, Ltr., Taylor to Clark, 16 June 1961. Available at: http://www.ndu.edu/library/taylor/taylorppr.html.

111. The Army position was that while the move from Pentomic division to ROAD was a move from a relatively new formation to "one that is familiar to nearly all Army personnel." Hence, extensively field testing was less of an issue in adopting the ROAD than it had been in the atomic division designs of the previous decade. NARA, RG 200, Record of Robert S. McNamara, Box 16, "A Study of the Proposed Reorganization of Army Divisions," undated, p.32.

112. Hawkins and Carafano, *Prelude to Army XXI*, p.17, Combat Studies Institute, "History of Transformation," *Military Review*, v.LXXX, n.3 (May-June 2000), pp.20-21, and Weigley, *History of the United States Army*, enlarged edition, pp.540-41.

113. This view was communicated to CONARC Commander General Herbert Powell by CSA George Decker upon his approval of the ROAD concept. Wilson, *Maneuver and Firepower*, p.298. Secretary of Defense McNamara, however, was still touting the ability to tailor the number of battalions in the division to President Kennedy the following January. NARA, RG 200, Record of Robert S. McNamara, Box 16, Memorandum to the President, re: Reorganization of Army Divisions, 2 January 1962.

114. After three years of inflation adjusted decline in defense spending in the later Eisenhower years, the DOD budget enjoyed 8.2% real growth in 1961 and 7.6% real growth in 1962. Active duty Army personnel increased from 873,000 in 1960 to 1,066,000 in 1962. Roger R. Trask and Alfred Goldberg, *The Department of Defense 1947-1997* (Washington, DC: Historical Office, Office of the Secretary of Defense, 1997), pp.169-71. Also see Weigley, *History of the United States Army*, enlarged edition, pp.538-39, 542-44. On the interest in counterinsurgency especially, see Andrew J. Birtle, *U.S. Army Counterinsurgency and Contingency Operations Doctrine 1942-1976* (Washington, DC: Center of Military History, 2006), chap.6.

115. Dastrup, *The US Army Command and General Staff College*, pp.110-11.

116. The Howze Board has been extensively examined elsewhere. See Ian Horwood, *Interservice Rivalry and Airpower in Vietnam* (Fort Leavenworth, KS: Combat Studies Institute, 2006), pp.30-47; Hamilton Howze, *A Cavalryman's Story: Memoirs of a Twentieth-Century Army General* (Washington, DC: Smithsonian Institution Press, 1996); Barbara A. Sorrill, *The Origins, Deliberations,*

and Recommendations of the U.S. Army Tactical Mobility Requirements Board (Fort Leavenworth, KS: Combat Developments Center, 1969); J. A. Stockfisch, *The 1962 Howze Board and Army Combat Developments* (Santa Monica, CA: RAND, 1994); LTG John J. Tolson, *Airmobility 1961-1971* (Washington, DC: Department of the Army, 1989), pp.20-24, and Wilson, *Maneuver and Firepower*, pp.314-18. Secretary of Defense McNamara's copy of the Howze Board report is located at NARA, RG 200, Record of Robert S. McNamara, Box 22.

117. For a succinct account of the intervention, see Roger J. Spiller, *"Not War But Like War": The American Intervention in Lebanon* (Fort Leavenworth, KS: Combat Studies Institute, 1981). For a recent treatment which deals with Eisenhower's broader approach to the Middle East, see Salim Yaqub, *Containing Arab Nationalism: The Eisenhower Doctrine in the Middle East* (Chapel Hill, NC: University of North Caroline Press, 2004).

118. It is this author's contention that one of Eisenhower's primary purposes in permitting Taylor to proceed with the Pentomic reorganization was primarily motivated by his long-term aims regarding US military assistance (especially regarding NATO Europe). US allies abroad (not just in NATO) often modeled their divisional structures on US tables of equipment. By creating a lighter US division with reduced tables of equipment, the US would have to provide less equipment to its Allies, hence decreasing its military aid expenditures and allowing the allied forces to better afford the projected forces that were called for in NATO defense plans. The Pentomic division should probably best be understood as a convergence of Army thinking about the need for units which could cope with the fluidity of a nuclear battlefield with President Eisenhower's interest in a smaller, lighter infantry division.

119. Of course, this was partially upset by the President's growing disenchantment with his senior military advisers. The Bay of Pigs fiasco particularly contributed to this problem. For a good overview, see H. R. McMaster, *Dereliction of Duty: Lyndon Johnson, Robert McNamara, the Joint Chiefs of Staff, and the Lies That Led to Vietnam* (New York: HarperCollins, 1997). Chapter 1 provides an overview of the relationship between the Kennedy administration and the JCS.

Chapter 2
Reorienting the Army–After Vietnam

The end of US involvement in the Vietnam War forced the Army to confront a host of issues which in many ways were even more daunting than those faced by the Army after the end of the Korean War. During the first three years of the Nixon administration, many of the challenges of transition were already garnering considerable attention from the President's national security apparatus, and increasingly from Congress as well. Writing to President Nixon in the fall of 1969 about the need to cut 4% from the FY 1970 defense budget, National Security Adviser Henry Kissinger noted that, "given the likelihood of continuing limits on defense spending . . . there will be intense competition among the Military Services for the limited resources," which "could lead to a return of the inter-Service battles of the 1950s and overwhelm any rational defense planning."[1] By 1973 the US Army faced a broad range of challenges as an institution seeking to rebuild from the painful denouement of its involvement in the Vietnam War.[2] Congressional pressure and economic realities did indeed entail reductions in defense spending (measured in constant dollars) in the first part of the 1970s. But the challenges the Army faced were not limited to the competition for scarce resources. Discipline and morale had slipped badly in the final years of the war; widespread drug use and racial tensions further undermined the Army. The year also witnessed two important institutional changes in the Army. First, Secretary of Defense Laird suspended the draft on 30 June 1973. The end of the draft was to have long-term implications for Army organization, recruitment, and self-conception. This presented the Army with new manpower difficulties that also had to be faced.[3] Second, the STEADFAST reorganization of 1973 did away with the Continental Army Command and replaced it with two new commands, Forces Command and Training and Doctrine Command, which are still in place today. Finally, the Yom Kippur War between Israel and the Arab states provided an opportunity to see the application of modern weaponry on the battlefield. The US Army seized upon this portent in its own efforts to reorient itself towards the traditional mission of defending Western Europe against a Soviet armored onslaught.

The Nixon Administration and Defense

When President Nixon came to office, he and his chief foreign policy advisor Henry Kissinger had a vision for American foreign policy in the

1970s.[4] Their ability to pursue that vision, however, rested in part on their ability to extricate the country from the Vietnam War. Nixon and Kissinger, well aware that the domestic mood pressed hard for the withdrawal of US forces, were determined to win a settlement in Vietnam which would not saddle the United States with the onus of having "lost" the war or abandoned its ally, South Vietnam. As a result of this conviction, the Nixon administration continued the US commitment to South Vietnam into 1973, ultimately with frustratingly little to show for it.[5] This ongoing commitment exacerbated economic difficulties the country was facing in the early 1970s, which created ever greater domestic and Congressional pressure for sharper cuts in the defense budget.

In the midst of the ongoing commitment to Vietnam, which domestically served to further undermine support for US deployments abroad, the Nixon administration was also undertaking the quintessential review of US strategy and military posture which characterized the first year of any US administration. The day after Nixon's inauguration, Kissinger directed—at the President's behest—that a study be prepared on US military posture and the balance of power which would present the implications on security and foreign policy for a range of different force levels.[6] By the fall of 1969, the national security apparatus had worked out a general posture for both strategic and general purpose forces. Nixon communicated the general lines of administration planning to Congress in the *First Annual Report to Congress on United States Foreign Policy for the 1970s.* Regarding strategic forces, the administration rejected either retreating to a "finite deterrence" posture or ramping up the production of strategic nuclear forces excessively, aiming to keep pace with the Soviets to maintain a rough parity. This was referred to as the strategy of "sufficiency."[7] In the realm of US overseas commitments, a significant shift in policy had been intimated in Nixon's informal remarks to reporters on Guam in July 1969. This statement, subsequently referred to as the Nixon Doctrine, signaled a retreat in the long-term from wide-ranging commitments throughout Asia and the Middle East.[8] Henceforth the United States would provide assistance to regional allies in Asia, but rely on them to provide the manpower. In Western Europe, by contrast, the Nixon administration reiterated their commitment to the existing strategy of flexible response, and promised to maintain US forces there at existing levels through "at least" mid-1971.[9] But even the long-term viability of this commitment would soon be challenged.

During 1969 the administration had operated under a defense budget determined in the final year of the Johnson administration. It was not until the FY 1971 budget was presented in early February 1970 that the fiscal impact of the Nixon administration's approach to defense emerged.[10] Though the proposed defense budget included slightly more than $5 billion in reductions, these came primarily from manpower reductions as a result of scaling back the US commitment in Southeast Asia. Congressional Democrats, led by Senator Mike Mansfield (D-MT), soon pressed for more drastic cuts. Melvyn Laird, who had served in the House of Representatives from 1952 to 1968 before agreeing to serve as Nixon's Secretary of Defense (the first Congressman to do so), worked hard to prune the defense budget in order to allay Congressional pressure for deeper cuts.[11] During the summer and fall of 1970 the administration struggled to counter the prevailing mood favoring steeper cuts.[12]

While the NSC bureaucracy began working out various options for defense postures, Secretary of Defense Laird developed a strategic concept of "realistic deterrence" which he believed would bring the defense budget in line with President Nixon's foreign policy goals. Laird presented his national security strategy report to President Nixon in November 1970.[13] Conforming to the policy goals of the administration, particularly the Nixon Doctrine and the President's *First Annual Report to the Congress of the United States on Foreign Policy*, Laird's report was titled, "A Strategy for Peace: A National Security Strategy of Realistic Deterrence." The study advocated a 1½ war concept in which the United States would maintain sufficient forces to fight a major conventional war (oriented especially towards Europe), while maintaining the capability for a "sub-theater" conflict elsewhere. Some of the most interesting departures in "A Strategy for Peace" were to be found in Laird's analysis of the "lessons learned" from Vietnam.[14] Laird wrote that the Johnson administration's mistake in its approach to "sub-theater hostilities" (such as counterinsurgency or guerilla warfare) had been to commit a "highly capable US conventional force, designed primarily for warfighting but deployed in increments to assume this type of burden."[15] He advocated that the future US force structure should be split, specifically in order to provide a new type of force structure for sub-theater hostilities. Laird thought it was "essential that we proceed down a different path in our planning for sub-theater hostilities." The key would be an "integrated team concept" including restructured US forces, forces of US allies, military and economic assistance, and a range of other diplomatic, political, and economic initiatives.[16] What would this mean for the Army? Laird proposed a force with the equivalent of thirteen active divisions and eight reserve divisions. This force would be split. Nine active and four reserve divisions would remain oriented towards theater warfighting capabilities and be primarily committed to Europe. The other four active and four reserve division *equivalents*, however, would be "brigades organized for special, quick response operations."[17] He wanted to see greater emphasis on "the concept of independent operations much more for these sub-theater forces than has been the case previously-including such aspects as integrated but not necessarily sophisticated tactical air capability, appropriate logistics, and improved defensive capabilities."[18] For Laird, it was important not to "subsume our sub-theater planning, either overall or for military forces, to the concept of homogenous, sophisticated, and theater-oriented capability."[19] This concept of splitting the force was never realized during Laird's tenure as Secretary of Defense (nor has it been subsequently). Nonetheless, the paper provided Laird with the "conceptual framework" for the FY 1972 and FY 1973 defense budgets which he supervised.[20]

The reasons why Secretary Laird's concept for developing a split force did not advance any farther are not entirely clear, however. The concept of dedicating a part of the Army force to sub-theater or regional contingency operations has only occasionally surfaced in the military literature.[21] The failure of Laird's concept to gain any traction may have to do with a number of factors. For one, Laird was not as disposed as Secretary Robert Mc-Namara had been to micro-manage the Department of Defense. In his FY 1971 annual defense report, he stated that he was "placing primary responsibility for detailed force planning on the Joint Chiefs and the Services, and we are delegating to the Military Departments more responsibility to manage development and procurement programs."[22] Laird had also made it clear upon becoming Secretary of Defense that he did not intend to serve beyond Nixon's first term.[23] With much of his attention focused on winding down US involvement in Vietnam and managing the defense budget, there was undoubtedly less time for the Secretary to follow-up on ideas for long-term force transformation. After Laird's retirement, he was succeeded briefly by Elliot Richardson, who served for a mere four months (January-May 1973) before President Nixon appointed him Attorney General. Richardson's successor, James Schlesinger, would prove a strong advocate of higher defense budgets, but this advocacy created friction with President Ford and eventually led to Schlesinger's dismissal from office in November 1975.[24] This considerable turn-over in civilian direction of the Secretary of Defense's office probably contributed to more autonomy on the part of the Joint Chiefs of Staff and the individual services.[25]

Within the institutional Army, there were clear trends away from "sub-theater" operations in the 1970s. Army Special Forces were reduced from 13,000 men in 1971 to 3,000 men in 1974.[26] Counterinsurgency was also

48

waning as part of the Army's curriculum in the 1970s. At CGSC there were still forty hours of instruction on counterinsurgency as late as 1977, but this fell to eight hours two years later.[27] The War College had dropped internal defense and development to two weeks instruction by 1972, and further reductions scaled even this limited instruction back to a mere two days by 1975.[28] All this helps explain why little seems to have come of Laird's suggestion for reorganizing part of the force for "sub-theater" operations.

Even the commitment of US forces to Europe remained far from certain in the turbulent early 1970s. There had been significant congressional pressure since late in the Johnson administration, spearheaded by Senator Mansfield, for reduced US force levels in Europe.[29] The criticism had been muted in 1967 when the US, Great Britain, and West Germany negotiated a Trilateral Agreement which dealt with the offset problem into 1968. Then in August 1968 the Soviet Union's invasion of Czechoslovakia again temporarily halted pressure for troop reductions.[30] General pressure for defense reductions and growing US international economic problems brought renewed Congressional pressure for reductions of US forces in Europe in 1969.[31] By late 1970, the National Security Council supported the view that it would be in the US interest, e.g. more conducive to public opinion, to convince the Europeans to strengthen their own forces, rather than spend money offsetting the costs of US troops deployed in Europe, particularly West Germany. This option was seen as a long-term goal (and indeed it had been a long-term US goal since the Eisenhower administration), but past experience with offset negotiations made it doubtful if it would find much support alliance wide.[32] "Burden sharing," as it was referred to in the NATO parlance, long remained a point of contention between the United States and its European allies.[33] In late November 1970, however, this long-term policy goal was deferred by the promulgation of National Security Decision Memoranda 95. This document stated that given the strategic balance between the US and the USSR, it was "vital that NATO have a credible conventional defense posture to deter and, if necessary, defend against conventional attack by Warsaw Pact forces." It called specifically for increased emphasis "given to defense by conventional forces."[34] This emphasis on conventional force defense would become a dominant motif of the 1976 edition of the Army's FM 100-5.

This defense was to be prepared to meet a full-scale conventional attack, on the presumption that warning time sufficient for mobilization had been given.[35] The emphasis on time for mobilization fitted with moves by Secretary of Defense Laird to integrate Reserve and National Guard units back into the "total force."[36] During the Johnson administration, the active Army had relied primarily on the draft and induced enlistments to maintain its manpower. With the projected reductions in US forces as involvement wound down in Vietnam and the long-term viability of the draft in question, the shift to greater reliance on reserve forces for future contingencies seemed to suggest an economical approach to manpower difficulties. However, the lack of combat experience (hence, questionable leadership skills), low levels of training, and obsolete equipment meant that there were significant challenges to be faced in this new policy. And this may have been the least of the challenges the post-Vietnam US Army had to face.

The STEADFAST Reorganization

There had been wide recognition in the Army, especially after the Nixon Doctrine was enunciated, that the post-Vietnam era would be one of retrenchment. As in the post-World War II and post-Korean War periods, attention turned to planning for the smaller Army of the future. The end of the Vietnam War would also mean the return of much of the Army to the continental United States, from which its ability to deploy quickly in combat situations would depend on the quality of training and readiness. Responsibility for troops in the continental US since 1955 had been vested in the Continental Army Command (CONARC). During the Vietnam War, there was growing concern about CONARC's ability to meet its wideranging mission. Two studies conducted during the Vietnam War, the Haines Board (on education) of 1966 and the Parker Panel of 1969 (an ad hoc committee initiated within the office of the Army Chief of Staff), both concluded that CONARC had too many roles and missions, and required reform.[37]

By December 1971, with troop withdrawals in Vietnam underway, Vice Chief of Staff General Bruce Palmer, Jr. approached Assistant Vice Chief Lieutenant General William E. DePuy and requested that he undertake a study of a possible reorganization of CONARC. DePuy and a small staff—often meeting confidentially on Saturday mornings—worked out a general plan for reorganization which was briefed in succession to Generals Palmer, Westmoreland, and Secretary of the Army Robert F. Froehlke between 27-29 January 1972. The plan, which was briefed as an "Impetus for Change," called for the disestablishment of CONARC and its replacement by two new commands: Forces Command (FORSCOM) and Training and Doctrine Command (TRADOC). Though the Army Staff and the Secretary were won over by DePuy and his staff's plan, it soon ran in

50

to considerable opposition from the Commanding General of CONARC, General Ralph Haines, Jr. One of the main issues that exercised Haines was the problem of dual control over installations in the CONUS, which if they included both active forces and training or education centers, would leave their installation commanders beholden to two masters. For Haines this threatened to violate the sacrosanct principle of "unity of command." Interestingly, Haines' concern would manifest itself at the end of the decade when TRADOC and FORSCOM had some difficulties collaborating on the establishment of the National Training Center.[38] Despite these objections, the reorganization drive gathered momentum in the Pentagon. By early March, DePuy had succeeded in getting Major General James G. Kalergis named Army Project Manager for Reorganization, and on 27 April Secretary of the Army Froehlke signed a charter authorizing the reorganization to proceed.[39]

The end of major periods of conflict traditionally provided a time for reflection and reorganization, and the end of US involvement in Vietnam was no different. The man called upon to direct that effort, prior to his unfortunate early death, was General Creighton Abrams. Abrams, who had been brought back from command of US forces in Vietnam by Secretary of Defense Laird to head the Army, was sworn in as Chief of Staff on 16 October 1972.[40] After being dispatched on a return trip to Vietnam to convince South Vietnamese President Thieu to accept the peace that Henry Kissinger was then brokering in Paris, Abrams next set out to assess the situation in Europe. There he discovered that the US Seventh Army was in shambles, the consequences of having been used as a forward rotating base during the war in Vietnam. Turning his attention to the leadership of the senior service schools, he stated that readiness was to be the central concern of the Army.[41] Acutely aware that this would be even more difficult given the sharp cutbacks in manpower, Abrams wanted to trim headquarters and staff sizes to help improve the 'tooth-to-tail' ratio of the active forces.[42]

Abrams maintained support for the Office of the Project Manager for Reorganization under the direction of Major General Kalergis. Kalergis was charged with a reorganization plan which gave substance to the outline DePuy's staff had developed and would "improve active and Reserve force readiness, make schools and training more effective, improve the methods of developing equipment and forces, streamline management, and reduce overhead." As a result of this study and its recommendations, a wide-ranging reorganization was announced by Secretary of the Army Froehlke and General Creighton W. Abrams on 11 January 1973.[43] The

1973 reorganization resulted in the dissolution of the Continental Army Command and the Combat Developments Command. The functions of these two commands were then redistributed to two new commands, the United States Army Forces Command (FORSCOM) and the United States Army Training and Doctrine Command (TRADOC). FORSCOM was responsible for all operational divisions and other forces in the continental United States, as well as the readiness of US Army Reserve and Army National Guard units. TRADOC was charged with overseeing all aspects of Army training and education, and the combat development process.[44]

One of the more interesting initiatives of Abrams' leadership was his announcement in March 1974 during a Congressional hearing that he aimed to establish a 16-division force. What made this surprising was that the force then budgeted was 13 and 2/3 divisions, and, if anything, the Army expected to face further reductions in strength. Abrams made this decision on his own, without supporting staff work. The decision, like much of Abrams' leadership as Chief of Staff, aimed to help stabilize the army and help restore perceptions of confidence in it, both externally and internally. The decision also meant that reserve readiness would be absolutely vital, because the 16-division force could not deploy without the mobilization of the Reserves.[45] This would serve as an implicit restraint on civilian policy makers, because dependence upon the use of the reserves would make both Congress and the executive branch aware that, "when the Army is committed, the American people are committed; when the American people lose their commitment it is futile to try and keep the Army committed."[46]

The Nixon administration embraced the reintegration of the National Guard and Reserves with the active Army into a Total Force, and Abrams' decision to develop a 16-division force posture further cemented this reunion.[47] To make this a workable concept it was critical for the Army to develop doctrine and training for the employment of this integrated force. The essential focus had been provided by the Nixon Doctrine and the administration's decision in NSDM 95 to ensure the capability for credible conventional deterrence in Europe. The public declaration by President Nixon, and National Security Adviser Henry Kissinger, of 1973 as the "Year of Europe" created an atmosphere in which the Army's turn to Europe fell in sync with the proclaimed foreign policy agenda.[48] The Army was quick to embrace this return to a more conducive and comfortable strategic environment.[49] This shift was reinforced by the widespread briefing of the Astarita Report throughout 1973-74.

General Abrams created a special Strategic Assessment Group in the spring of 1973 to determine what role there was for conventional forces after the Vietnam War.[50] The Strategic Assessment Group was headed by Abrams' confidant Colonel Edward F. Astarita. While the group prepared their report in the spring and summer of 1973, they were supervised by Abrams and Major General Roland Hiaser, the Deputy Chief of Staff for Operations Plans Directorate. Consonant with the Nixon Doctrine, the report saw the reassurance of America's traditional allies in Western Europe and also Japan as priorities. Given tensions within NATO and economic competition between Western Europe and the United States, the report identified that "the problem for the foreseeable future is the survivability of the United States–West European alliance."[51] Reflecting the climate of the times, the report recognized that the past rationale of "defending Western Europe from communist hordes" was unlikely to resonate when détente and summitry had "drastically eroded public perception of the threat."[52] The report specifically addressed this problem of public perception by pointing out that conventional forces played an important role in national strategy for a number of reasons. It endorsed the role of conventional forces in flexible response (officially embraced in NATO strategy in 1967-68) as enhancing the deterrent. Implicit in this was the old Army line, running back to Ridgway and Taylor, that greater conventional forces strengthened the credibility of US deterrence:

> This assurance of allies is a primary role of conventional forces. . . .
>
> *   *   *   *   *   *   *
>
> The higher the credibility of such assurances, the higher the probability of the use of strategic nuclear retaliatory forces to protect allies, the higher is American freedom of action and freedom from coercion in international relations.[53]

While the report virtually conceded that strategic nuclear deterrence was the purview of the Air Force and the Navy, it pointed out that while sufficient conventional forces-in-being were not created to provide the capability for rapid conflict termination—"an unlikely contingency in the foreseeable future"—a "full range of nuclear options is necessary." Again, one might well see in a "full range of nuclear options" a harkening back to the arguments advanced for tactical nuclear weapons in the Pentomic era. But this was hedged by the claim that Army forces, because of the ability to deploy significant firepower at "the lower end of the spectrum," in times of "crisis they [Army forces] are less escalatory." It also suggested that while the Air Force and Navy's greater mobility gave them the capability for rapid response, because the Army's deployments were more ponderous, they demonstrated a greater level of commitment.[54]

Repeatedly throughout its conclusions, the Astarita Report emphasized that future Army forward deployments would be justified on the basis of the themes of assurance and deterrence. Given the public mood after Vietnam, it was important for the Army to have the backing and support of the American people.[55] Indeed, the success of the military strategy advanced in the Astarita Report was dependent upon "the will, the resolve, and the determination of the American people to carry it out."[56] When critics charged that the report merely legitimized the status quo, General Fred Weyand replied that the report had served as "a real eyeopener" which showed that the Army had been following a sound military policy, with its forward deployments "reinforcing our foreign policy objectives in these critical areas."[57] Ultimately the Astarita Report demonstrated greater concern for selling the Army's mission to the American public than identifying a need for reform.

The Arab-Israeli War of October 1973 provided the catalyst for the refocused attention on the European battlefield.[58] It was easy to see the Yom Kippur War as a microcosm of potential conflict in Europe, if one ignored the awkward problem of whether or not tactical nuclear weapons would be used on the European battlefield (of which there were 7,000 deployed in NATO Europe by the late 1960s). The Arab forces were Soviet equipped and trained. The Israeli force had American equipment, and relied on a highly trained force supported by rapidly mobilized reserves. This created a situation which seemed highly analogous to that which the NATO nations faced in Central Europe should conflict there somehow remain limited to a conventional exchange.[59] The US Army quickly dispatched a number of teams to Israel in the aftermath of the war to absorb its "lessons." This included a team led by Colonel Prillaman of the Armor School, one led by General Talbott from TRADOC, a US Military Operations Team, a USAF team, a USMC team, and a visit by S.L.A. Marshall.[60] In order to compile the mass of detail, General Abrams instructed TRADOC to provide a single assessment.[61] While the TRADOC assessment was being compiled, TRADOC's new commander, General William E. DePuy, prepared his own short analysis of the lessons learned.[62] In the course of eighteen days of fighting both the Israelis and the Arab forces lost enormous amounts of equipment. For DePuy this demonstrated that "modern weapons are vastly more lethal than any weapons we have encountered on the battlefield before." In order to prepare for these conditions, it was imperative to develop "highly trained and highly skilled combined arms teams."[63]

54

Doctrinal Ferment

In the midst of the post-Vietnam transition and the "lesson learning" from the Yom Kippur War, Army Chief of Staff General Abrams was repeatedly hospitalized for complications stemming from the removal of a cancerous lung.[64] He died in office on 4 September 1974, and was replaced by General Fred C. Weyand, who had served under Abrams as Vice Chief of Staff since 1973. During Weyand's years as Chief of Staff, DePuy became the driving force behind using TRADOC and doctrinal change as the most effective means of transforming the Army.[65] During 1974 TRADOC was focused on comparing existing US weapons systems against the implications of the Yom Kippur War. After a joint TRADOC-FORSCOM seminar in October 1974—dubbed OCTOBERFEST—which focused on the company-battery level combat on the modern battlefield, it became increasingly apparent to DePuy and his TRADOC staff that there was a need to "reorient and restructure the whole body of Army doctrine from top to bottom." They "perceived that the key would have to be the substantial revision of FM 100-5-Operations."[66] This process, initially intended to be complete by mid-1975, stretched into the summer of 1976.

When completed, this new version of FM 100-5 became known as Active Defense. In its opening pages on US Army Objectives (Chapter 1), the manual made passing reference to the notion of full-spectrum capabilities, but stressed that "battle in Central Europe against forces of the Warsaw Pact is the most demanding mission the US Army could be assigned." Reflecting DePuy's interpretation of the Yom Kippur War, the manual also pointed out that the "first battle of our next war could well be its last battle." This led to the conclusion that, "today the US Army must, above all else, prepare to win the first battle of the next war." Subsequently the manual's focus on defense and firepower at the expense of offensive initiative and maneuver would draw its strongest criticisms. This set the stage for another round of revisions after DePuy's retirement which would lead to the development of the 1982 FM 100-5 edition, known as AirLand Battle.[67]

But perhaps more troubling, if one were in fact interested in the Army's full-spectrum capabilities, was the extent to which the manual had become focused exclusively on the Central European battlefield to the exclusion of all else. For instance, chapters on Unconventional Warfare, Military Operations against Irregular Forces, Situations Short of War, Cold War Operations, and Stability Operations, which had been featured in the 1962 and

1968 manuals disappeared altogether. Chapter 14: "Military Operations in Special Environments" of the 1976 edition, the lone chapter which bucked this trend, focused on climatic zones such as jungles, deserts, mountains, northern regions, and briefly, urban environments. Even this chapter, however, was focused on special regions of NATO responsibility and the Middle East. In many ways Active Defense was entirely in line with historian George Herring's view that the country had suffered collective amnesia regarding the Vietnam War, but did provide a focus—though decidedly narrow—for the Army in the difficult years after Vietnam.

Part and parcel with the rewriting of doctrine, TRADOC also aimed to bring about a revolution in training to ensure that the peacetime Army was prepared for the "first battle" when it came. The 1976 edition of FM 100-5 stated that "training development must provide training standards and techniques *matched closely to the realities of the modern battlefield* [emphasis in original]."[68] Training problems had been one of many perceived deficiencies highlighted by the frustrations of Vietnam. General Westmoreland had authorized the creation of a CONARC Board for Dynamic Training in September 1971 to investigate those deficiencies. After the STEADFAST reorganization, responsibility for training became one of TRADOC's chief responsibilities. General DePuy's deputy for training from October 1973 was Major General Paul Gorman, who had served as President of the Board for Dynamic Training at Fort Benning from 1970-1971. Gorman and the Combat Arms Training Board, successor to the Board for Dynamic Training, used the performance based training model developed at Fort Benning to develop the Army Training and Evaluation Program (ARTEP). The ARTEP system required individual units to perform up to certain standards, based on conditions that would be experienced in combat, in order to become certified.[69] This replaced the older Army Training Program (ATP) which merely required a certain number of hours of training, but had no performance based evaluation feedback loop.

While ARTEP introduced an important measure of performance measurement in Army training, the increased range of weapons and scope of the modern battlefield presented the US Army with another training challenge. Most existing Army facilities in the 1970s lacked sufficient training space to allow units the size of battalions and larger to maneuver realistically.[70] The Navy and Air Force had already moved towards more realistic training systems for their pilots as a result of poor performance in the skies over Vietnam. The Naval Fighter Weapons School, or "Top Gun," had been established in 1969, and the Air Force was practicing force-on-force exercises (RED FLAG) at Nellis Air Force Base in Nevada. The Army favored the creation of an exercise range where force-on-force exercises could be conducted. In late 1976, Major General Gorman initiated the campaign for the creation of large-scale training centers for the Army.[71] By December 1977, FORSCOM and TRADOC had agreed, not without some friction, on plans for a National Training Center (NTC). It would be several years before the planning and budgetary hurdles could be overcome. When the National Training Center did at last open in 1980 at Fort Irwin, California, it provided the realistic large-unit training against the dedicated, Warsaw Pact-styled Opposing Force. This provided the level and realism in training that Army reformers had advocated throughout the 1970s.[72]

The NTC was formally established in October 1980, and Fort Irwin re-activated the following summer.[73] Once the NTC was activated, the Opposing Force would style themselves as the 32d Guards Motorized Rifle Regiment. In addition to using Soviet doctrine and training, they wore mock Soviet uniforms and drove M551 Sheridan light tanks modified to look like Soviet armored reconnaissance vehicles.[74] The first battalion force-on-force training against the Opposing Force was conducted in early October 1982.[75] Technological innovation also played an important role in the development of realistic training at the NTC. The Multiple Integrated Laser Engagement System (MILES) developed by Xerox Electro-Optical has been described by TRADOC historian Ann Chapman as "one of the twin technological foundations of the post-Vietnam training revolution."[76] It provided a realistic means of registering hits and kills in the force-on-force maneuvers which was a major leap over past maneuvers where neutral observers had scored hits based on subjective observation. To complement the NTC, in August 1985 a Center for Army Lessons Learned (CALL) was established at Fort Leavenworth, Kansas. CALL's mission was to collect and disseminate lessons to the active and Reserve components of the Army from combat experienced by the US and foreign armies, and from exercises conducted at the NTC and elsewhere.[77]

Meeting the Army's Educational Needs

There was a sense that the Army's educational institutions (West Point, CGSC, and the Army War College) needed to play more active roles in the adaptation of the Army to challenges of the post-Vietnam era. Throughout the 1970s, the Army education system was subjected to the scrutiny of numerous reviews and studies. The STEADFAST reorganizations also had important bearing on the educational system. One of the fortunate outgrowths of this reflective trend was a renewed interest in the study of military history within the Army. In 1967, CSA General Harold Johnson had approved a request for the establishment of a library and research collection at the Army War College. The collection was designated the US Army Military History Research Collection (now the Military History Institute). It has grown into one of the Army's premier centers for the study of military history.[78] The following year West Point added a Department of History. Though there was a long-established tradition of historical instruction at West Point, the newly formed department signaled the growing "organizational cachet" for the discipline.[79] At the behest of retiring Chief of Military History Brigadier General Hal C. Pattison, in 1971 General Westmoreland also formed a committee to inquire into the state of military history instruction in the US Army as a whole. The committee was chaired by Colonel Thomas E. Griess, Professor and Head of the newly formed Department of History at West Point.[80] It recommended strengthening history instruction systematically throughout the career arc of officers, to "develop historical mindedness among the officer corps at large."[81] As an outgrowth, the AWC and West Point both added visiting civilian history faculty in 1972, with CGSC following suit in 1974. The initial appointees were Theodore Ropp at the AWC, Jay Luvaas at West Point, and Harry L. Coles at CGSC.[82] General Westmoreland also encouraged the War College to serve as a "center for contemporary military thought."[83] He made use of the faculty and students at the War College to carry out a number of studies. These included a "Professionalism Study," "Leadership for the 1970's," and "Army Tasks for the Seventies."[84]

The Command and General Staff College was also undergoing important changes in the 1970s. These included reform of the CGSC curriculum, reorganization of the college's departments, and a campaign to award masters degree to its graduates. The latter campaign initially was encouraged by Major General Harold K. Johnson, commandant from August 1960 to February 1963. His initiative, however, stalled until Congressional approval to award a Masters of Military Arts and Sciences finally came in 1974.[85] Part and parcel with the program to award masters degrees and gain accreditation for CGSC was a reform of the curriculum. During the 1972-73 academic year a substantial number of electives were added to the curriculum, a process which continued throughout the remainder of the decade. All officers attending Leavenworth took a common core of courses on staff work, the fundamentals of tactics at the division, corps, and field army level, joint and combined operations, and defense and security assistance. These were complemented by professional and associated electives.[86] The professional electives allowed the officers to pursue branch related specialties, while the associated electives provided the broader

58

curriculum essential for accreditation. The changes helped contribute to a growing sense of professionalism at Leavenworth in the 1970s, but did not in themselves completely satisfy criticism of the Army's training and educational establishment.

Congressional and executive (from the Office of Management and Budget) pressure in 1976 and 1977 aimed at reducing the Army's training establishment.[87] Within the Army, there was concern that existing education and training programs "were not yet producing officers with the desired level of military competency." CSA General Meyer responded to this situation by initiating a Review of Education and Training of Officers (RETO) study in late August 1977. The study group was placed under the direction of Brigadier General Benjamin Harrison and reported directly to the Chief of Staff. The RETO study was wide-ranging in its scope. It examined the system for training and educating officers along the entire arc of their careers. The RETO study was conducted by a team of approximately 30 junior officers, who received input and conducted interviews of over 100 general officers. In addition, 14,000 officers provided survey data to the study team. The conclusions of the study were presented to General Meyer in late June 1978. Reflecting the sense of a commanding Warsaw Pact advantage in quantity of men and equipment, the RETO study pointed out that "the difference between victory and defeat will likely lie in the difference between the quality of our people and those of the enemy."[88]

The RETO Study made a great many recommendations, many of which would eventually be implemented.[89] Among them was the recommendation that a Combined Arms Services Staff School (CAS³) be created at Fort Leavenworth so that all Active Army and Reserve Component majors could receive training for serving on staffs.[90] All attendees would complete a 120-hour course packet before attending in residence for nine weeks. With this universalist approach to instruction in staff duties, the RETO Study recommended that attendance in the standard CGSC 42-week course be reduced from 40% to 20% of the eligible annual crop of officers.[91] This reduction was necessary in part to free resources for the CAS³. The CAS³ was established with an initial class of 120 students at Fort Leavenworth in April 1981, with continued expansion thereafter until all captains could attend between their seventh and ninth years of service.[92]

During the fall of 1978, TRADOC Commander General Donn Starry and Combined Arms Center (CAC) Commander Lieutenant General John Thurman III began to press for the development of a department of applied historical research at Fort Leavenworth. Starry and Thurman were initially interested in "historical investigations of Army doctrinal matters." Both were influenced, in part, by the recent publication of Trevor N. Dupuy's *A Genius for War: The German Army and the General Staff 1807-1945*, which demonstrated the important role of the German *Kriegakademie* in providing "the focal point of the intellectual investigation of doctrine."[93] A number of names for the new department were floated, including "Tactical Studies Institute," "Military History Institute for Combat Analysis," and "Combat Studies Institute." The latter was ultimately chosen for the new department, which was split off from the small cell of military history instructors then in the Department of Unified and Combined Arms at CGSC. The Combat Studies Institute (CSI) was formally established on 1 July 1979.[94] In its initial iteration, CSI served both as the department of military history of the Command and General Staff College, and as a center for research and publication on matters related to the tactical level of warfare.[95] Aptly suited to the mission General Starry and Lieutenant General Thurman had in mind, the first of the Leavenworth Papers (CSI's original publication series) was Major Robert A. Doughty's *The Evolution of US Army Tactical Doctrine, 1946-76*. Over the coming decades CSI represented an important element of the reflective, analytical trend that was institutionalized in the post-Vietnam War US Army.

The Army War College, especially under the direction of Major General DeWitt Smith, Jr., commandant from 1978 to 1980, was an important center of the Army's attempt to learn lessons from the Vietnam experience. The first effort in this regard was an elective course in the 1975-76 curriculum taught by Colonel Dwight L. Adams titled "The Vietnam War: Lessons Learned."[96] More ambitiously, Commandant Smith initiated a "Viet Nam Lessons Learned Study" that began under the auspices of the Strategic Studies Institute. Smith's project received support from VCSA General Walter Kerwin, Jr., but strong opposition was mounted by other elements of the Army Staff.[97] Because of its extensive scope, the study was eventually turned over to the BDM Corporation. They produced the eight volume "A Study of Strategic Lessons Learned in Vietnam," which was completed in June 1980. This extensive, critical study was effectively buried, however, when the Army readily embraced an alternate interpretation of the strategic lessons of the Vietnam War produced the following year by Colonel Harry Summers, Jr.[98]

Colonel Harry Summers, Jr. had been a member of the Astarita Study. In July 1979, he joined the Army War College faculty. While there Colonel Summers completed an assessment of American military involvement in

Vietnam, which he had begun while distilling findings of the BDM Corporations' multivolume study of the Vietnam War while serving on the Army Staff from 1975 to 1979.[99] His study received widespread distribution and comment, first as a publication of the Strategic Studies Institute under the title *On Strategy: The Vietnam War in Context*, and the following year as an imprint of Presidio Books as *On Strategy: A Critical Analysis of the Vietnam War*.[100] Summers' book rejected the BDM study's conclusions that the Army had performed poorly in Vietnam because of its failure to switch from conventional warfighting to a more appropriate low-intensity conflict strategy. For Summers, the Army won all its battles, but lost the war for two reasons. First, the Army had lost sight of the important Clausewitzian trinity that maintained a balance between the people, the government, and the Army. Summers saw it as essential for Army strategic planning to have public and Congressional support (this point was already evident in the Astarita Report).[101] A number of critics have seen this essentially as a manifestation of the Army's determination to "never again" get caught in a Vietnam-type situation.[102] Second, Summers argued that the Army had abrogated its role in the determination of strategy. It was important that the Army do more than simply "design and procure material, arms, and equipment and to organize, train, and equip soldiers." This limited view of the Army's mission led to a "regression in military thought." Instead, it was essential for the Army to articulate a military strategy.[103] The President, in Summers' view, was not to formulate military strategy, but decide on options presented to him by his military and civilian advisers. This in turn seemed to implicitly criticize the micromanagement of military conduct of the Vietnam War which had characterized the Johnson administration writ large, and the McNamara Pentagon especially. Summers' version of Vietnam's lessons would be codified in the 1984 Weinberger Doctrine. The language of the Weinberger Doctrine owed a good deal to the contributions of Secretary of Defense Weinberger's Military Assistant, Major General Colin Powell, and was in essence a simplified version of Summers' *On Strategy*.[104]

The Strategic Studies Institute (SSI) had emerged in the late 1970s as one of the Army's pre-eminent think tanks devoted to strategy. Formerly the Institute of Advanced Studies, SSI returned to the Army War College fold as part of the STEADFAST reorganization.[105] Thereafter it served as a "field agency" for the Deputy Chief of Staff of Operations and Strategy, who in turn was given supervisory authority over both the War College and SSI. SSI was also one of the few agencies within the Army that emerged from the STEADFAST reorganization with an authorized higher manning level.[106] Following the successful development of *Parameters* as the War

College's regular journal in 1970, SSI began to publish a series of *Military Issue Research Memorandums*. In 1975 they published *New Dynamics of National Strategy: The Paradox of Power*, which was the results of a symposium on security issues held the previous year.[107] When the US Army embraced the concept of operations art in the early 1980s, the Strategic Studies Institute played an important role in disseminating pertinent material, especially through publications of its Art of War Colloquium.[108]

Towards Army 86

Renewed concern with the Warsaw Pact threat and the example of modern war in the 1973 Arab-Israeli conflict also prompted concern in the US Army about whether or not the ROAD division was optimally suited for the challenges of anticipated warfare in Europe. A TRADOC study in 1975 reported that the Army's divisions were inadequate to meet their Warsaw Pact opponents.[109] Senator Sam Nunn of Georgia was also pressuring the Army to review its capabilities to meet a quick, massive Warsaw Pact assault on NATO forces on the Central Front. As a result of Nunn's pressure, CSA General Weyand dispatched Lieutenant General James Hollingsworth, who had been serving as a corps commander in Korea, on an inspection trip to Europe in the spring of 1976. Hollingsworth was reportedly critical of USAEUR's defense plans and concluded that "the direct conventional defense capability for Central Europe is not credible today."[110] In response to these trends which reinforced preoccupation with the European battlefield, the Army Staff authorized TRADOC to undertake another divisional restructuring study in March 1976.[111] TRADOC then established the Divisional Restructuring Study (DRS) Group on 4 May. Within six weeks a preliminary divisional concept was briefed to General Weyand that called for retention of the traditional three brigade structure, but with heavier brigades.[112] Weyand's successor as Chief of Staff, General Bernard Rogers, authorized the 1st Cavalry Division to carry out a Division Restructuring Evaluation in early 1977.[113]

The one year test evaluation for the 1st Cavalry Division met resistance within the Army. It was considered to be too rushed, and was instead rolled into a longer-term study which became known as Division 86. This more measured redesign effort was strongly supported by General Donn Starry, DePuy's successor as TRADOC commander.[114] This would ultimately result in the Heavy Division 86 design. It called for a division with nearly 20,000 personnel and the edition of an organic attack helicopter maneuver brigade (making four brigades altogether) within the division. Though it was approved in principle in 1980 by then Chief of Staff General Edward C. Meyer, Heavy Division 86 proved to be an unrealistic goal by the mid-1980s. Though the Army and military establishment generally had benefitted from the increased budgetary appropriations of the late Carter and early Reagan years, Heavy Division 86 proved too expensive to implement. In addition, the 1980s saw a resurgence of interest in light, deployable infantry to deal with contingency operations. The invasion of Grenada in Operation URGENT FURY in 1983 was seen as an important early example of the utility of rapidly deployable light infantry.[115]

Operational Art and AirLand Battle

Since the early 1980s the US Army has stressed thinking about the operational art of warfare, especially the conduct of joint warfare campaigns. In part this emphasis on the operational art grew out of dissatisfaction with the 1976 edition of FM 100-5, especially the feeling that it was overly preoccupied with the "first battle" and the tactics of defensive warfare. The revival of Clausewitz specifically, and the German approach to mechanized warfare generally, led to the introduction of the Russian/German conception of a third level of warfare, referred to as operational art, between the level of tactics and strategy.[116] Growing emphasis from within and outside the military on joint operations, especially contingency plans, stimulated the revival of campaign plans and interest in operations beyond mere battlefield tactics. The failure at Desert One, the attempted rescue of US hostages in Iran in April 1980, also increased interest in improving the joint planning process.

In the summer of 1979, General Edward Meyer, shortly to become CSA, informed TRADOC commander General Donn Starry that it would be appropriate to begin preparation of a new edition of FM 100-5.[117] In August 1982 the new edition of FM 100-5 was published.[118] While the 1976 edition had been geared toward the "first battle" that DePuy deemed so critical, the 1982 edition stressed the need to fight and win not just battles, but implicitly *campaigns* as well. This meant greater attention would be paid to operations, not just the tactics of defense that had been prominent in the previous edition. Two of the authors of the new doctrine wrote: "the operational concept of FM 100-5 is the central idea of the manual."[119] It also explicitly stressed the offensive, advocating that the Army must "retain the initiative and disrupt our opponent's fighting capability in depth with deep attack, effective firepower, and decisive maneuver."[120] General Starry had presented the concepts of deep attack and extended battlefield the previous year in his article, "Extending the Battlefield."[121] Sounding a note which resonated with the conclusions that Colonel Summers had reached, Starry wrote:

> The concept [extended battlefield] emphasizes the all too frequently ignored or misunderstood lesson of history that once political authorities commit military forces in pursuit of political aims, military forces must win something, or else there will be no basis from which political authorities can bargain to win politically. Therefore, the purpose of military operations cannot be simply to avert defeat [ala Vietnam], but, rather, it must be to win.[122]

One of the other striking features of Starry's presentation was the extent to which tactical nuclear weapons, and to an extent chemical weapons, again figured into the Army's conception of a future battlefield. Breaking with the deterrent concept of tactical nuclear weapons as then understood in the NATO context, Starry wrote that "Theater forces should not be considered solely as a bridge to strategic nuclear war. They are weapons which must be considered in the context of a war-fighting capability."[123]

This renewed emphasis on theater nuclear weapons was part of a larger debate going on within NATO over the modernization of theater nuclear capabilities and attempts to define rules for the employment of tactical nuclear weapons.[124] Within the Army, there was indeed a revival of discussion of theater nuclear warfare.[125] One example of this renewed enthusiasm for thinking about the tactical nuclear battlefield was John P. Rose's *The Evolution of U.S. Army Nuclear Doctrine, 1945-1980*. Originally a dissertation at the University of Southern California (it was reprinted in a limited edition by Westview Press), Rose's book was written out of "a sense of urgency," reflecting the need "to train our soldiers on how to fight, survive and win in a nuclear environment."[126] By the middle of the decade, an updated field manual titled *Nuclear Weapons Employment Doctrine and Procedures* had been produced.[127] Like its earlier incarnation in the Pentomic era, the 1980s discussion over tactical nuclear battlefields would eventually peter out in the same strategic dead end of the earlier generation of thought.[128] Progress towards nuclear arms control between Reagan and Gorbachev played a significant role in curtailing the debate as well; in December 1987 Intermediate-range Nuclear Force (INF) Treaty was signed which called for the elimination of all long and short-range missiles from the European continent.[129] With progress being made on nuclear arms reduction, it seemed natural that conventional force reductions would soon follow.[130]

The emphasis on deep battle and interdiction in the 1982 FM 100-5

64

had long term implications for the Army's training and educational programs. But in the practical realm, a decade after the end of the Vietnam War, the US military was to find itself facing the greatest challenge once again from the problem of low intensity warfare. As the country began to shake off the long shadow of the Vietnam War, the US military again found itself being called upon to provide troops for contingency operations and in support of low-intensity conflict, especially in Latin America. To its credit, the 1982 AirLand Battle edition of FM 100-5 had included chapters on Joint, Contingency, and Combined Operations, but these three chapters were added to the end of the manual, giving them a distinctly appended feel. AirLand Battle doctrine was refined in an edition of FM 100-5 in 1986. It remained the Army's approach to warfighting until the concept was dropped after the end of the Cold War.[131]

Institutionally AirLand Battle's emphasis on the operational art of war found expression in the establishment in the School of Advanced Military Studies (SAMS) at Fort Leavenworth. Lieutenant Colonel Huba Wass de Czege, who had served on the doctrine writing team for the 1982 FM 100-5, was an important proponent of adding a second-year of instruction to the CGSC curriculum for select graduates.[132] Building on the analysis of the RETO Study, a Strategic Studies Institute "Planner Study," and a review of CGSC by Major General Guy S. Meloy III, Wass de Czege argued that the amount of tactical instruction at Fort Leavenworth had decreased precipitously since the 1950s.[133] In addition, the emphasis on training, rather than a broad education in the principles of war, had the danger of creating an Army that was ill-prepared to conceive and anticipate future challenges. To rectify these problems, Wass de Czege advocated institutionalizing the pilot Advanced Military Studies Program that had been initiated in 1982. This would mean that by 1990 there were 288 majors and 180 lieutenant colonels who had received the additional year of instruction in operational planning.[134] It became a one-year course in the School of Advanced Military Studies the following year.[135] AirLand Battle and the first generation of SAMS planners were given their baptismal test in the first Gulf War. Both were generally perceived within the Army to have performed admirably.[136]

Summary

In the era of difficult transition and adaptation that marked the close of direct US involvement in Southeast Asia and the reorientation towards NATO and the European battlefield, the US Army experienced a decidedly reflective time. At the beginning of its post-Vietnam transition, one potential path towards adaptation which would have called for the splitting of the Army into two functionally specialized forces was suggested by then Secretary of Defense Melvin Laird. This functional split would have provided for about two-thirds of the Army to orient itself towards large-scale theater war, while the remaining one-third became a specialized, highly-mobile force based on brigades geared towards contingency (or "sub-theater" as Laird referred to them) operations elsewhere in the world. This path seemingly garnered little support outside the Office of the Secretary of Defense, and became a footnote to history. Given the challenges of converting the Army to an All-Volunteer Force and dealing with the personnel problems which characterized the Vietnam-era US Army, it was perhaps a goal beyond the capabilities of the institutional Army at the time to embrace in any case.

What emerged instead was an institution that prepared itself up almost exclusively for the mission that seemed to provide both the greatest and the most traditional challenge, large-scale theater warfare. Over the course of the decade, leadership from men such as CSA General Creighton Abrams, and TRADOC commanders General William E. DePuy and General Donn Starry guided the institutional Army towards its renewed and tightly focused mission. To a greater extent than was the case in the 1950s, the Army turned towards formalized institutions to aid in this process. The establishment of TRADOC with its emphasis on realistic training and a doctrinally based force exemplified this trend. The emergence of the National Training Center, Strategic Studies Institute, Combat Studies Institute, School of Advanced Military Studies, and the Center for Army Lessons Learned were all symptomatic of the degree to which "lesson learning" and historical and strategic reflection became institutionalized in the post-Vietnam era. The growth of this institutionalized learning process is still a part of the Army today.

Notes

1. NARA, Nixon Presidential Material, NSC Institutional ("H") Files, National Security Study Memorandums, Box H-128, Memorandum for the President, re: September 10 [1969] NSC Meeting, undated.

2. There is a large volume of scholarly literature on American involvement in Vietnam. Among the better studies are Phillip B. Davidson, *Vietnam at War: The History 1946-1975* (New York: Oxford University Press, 1991); George C. Herring, *America's Longest War: The United States and Vietnam, 1950-1975*, 3rd edition (New York: McGraw Hill, 1996); David E. Kaiser, *American Tragedy: Kennedy, Johnson, and the Origins of the Vietnam War* (Cambridge, MA: Belknap Press of Harvard University Press, 2000); Fredrik Logevall, *Choosing War: The Lost Chance for Peace and the Escalation of War in Vietnam* (Berkeley, CA: University of California Press, 1999); H. R. McMaster, *Dereliction of Duty*; and Robert D. Schulzinger, *A Time for War: The United States and Vietnam, 1941-1975* (New York: Oxford University Press, 1997). A number of fine volumes have also been produced by the Center for Military History in both their Vietnam Studies series, available at: http://www.history.army.mil/html/bookshelves/collect/vn-studies.html and the official *The United States Army in Vietnam* series. The ninth and most recent volume in the series is Graham A. Cosmas, *MACV: The Joint Command in the Years of Escalation 1962-1967* (Washington, DC: Center of Military History, United States Army, 2006).

3. Richard Lock-Pullan has recently argued that the end of the draft more than the end of US involvement in the war itself; or changes in technology; or changes in the strategic environment, shaped the nature of the US Army after 1973. This was because the end of the draft presented a challenge to the Army's self-conception as the nation-in-arms. Richard Lock-Pullan, "'An Inward Looking Time': The United States Army, 1973-1976," *The Journal of Military History*, v.67, n.2 (April 2003), p.484, and Lock-Pullan, *US Army Intervention Policy and Army Innovation*, pp.49-51. General Westmoreland as Chief of Staff urged the Nixon administration to "keep a selective service law on the books," even if the draft itself was rescinded. William C. Westmoreland, *A Soldier Reports* (Garden City, NY; Doubleday & Company, 1976), p.455. Also see James F. Dunnigan and Raymond M Macedonia, *Getting It Right: American Military Reforms After Vietnam to the Gulf War and Beyond* (New York: William Morrow & Co., 1993), pp.143-56; Robert K. Griffith, *The U.S. Army's Transition to the All-Volunteer Force, 1968-1974* (Washington, DC: US Army Center of Military History, 1997), passim; and Richard Stewart, gen. ed., *American Military History*, vol.II: *The United States Army in a Global Era, 1917-2003* (Washington, DC; Center of Military History, 2005), p.369.

4. Melvin Small, *The Presidency of Richard Nixon* (Lawrence, KS: University Press of Kansas, 1999), pp.94-125 takes a favorable view of Nixon's ap-

proach to the Soviet Union and China, crediting with the diplomatic openings which "marked the beginning of the end of the cold war." For a more critical view of Nixon era foreign policy, see William Bundy, *A Tangled Web: The Making of Foreign Policy in the Nixon Presidency* (New York: Hill and Wang, 1998). Most recently the President and his National Security Advisor have been the subject of Robert Dallek's *Nixon and Kissinger: Partners in Power* (New York: Harper Collins, 2007). There is a great deal of detail on the mechanics of US-Soviet negotiations, including arms control talks, in Raymond L. Garthoff, *Détente and Confrontation: American-Soviet Relations from Nixon to Reagan* (Washington, DC: The Brookings Institution, 1985). Two other recent studies contribute to our understanding of the role of Henry Kissinger in the Nixon administration's foreign policy. See Jussi Hanhimäki, *The Flawed Architect: Henry Kissinger and American Foreign Policy* (Oxford: Oxford University Press, 2004), and Jeremi Suri, *Henry Kissinger and the American Century* (Cambridge, MA: Belknap Press, 2007). Though they are not unproblematic, there is a wealth of information in Kissinger's three volumes of memoirs on the Nixon-Ford years: *White House Years* (Boston: Little, Brown and Company, 1979), *Years of Upheaval* (Boston: Little, Brown and Company, 1982), and *Years of Renewal* (New York: Simon and Schuster, 1999).

5. George C. Herring, *America's Longest War: The United States and Vietnam, 1950-1975*, 3rd edn. (New York: McGraw Hill, 1996), pp.243-47.

6. Nixon Library (Online), National Security Study Memorandum [hereafter NSSM] 3, 21 January 1969. Available online at http://www.nixonlibrary.gov/virtuallibrary/documents/nationalsecuritymemoranda.php.

7. *First Annual Report to the Congress on the United States Foreign Policy for the 1970's*. 18 February 1970.

8. Robert Dallek, *Nixon and Kissinger*, pp.143-44. Also Don Oberdorfer, "U.S. Bars New Asia War Role," *The Washington Post*, 26 July 1969, p.A1; and Robert B. Semple, Jr., "Nixon Plans Cut in Military Role for U.S. in Asia," *New York Times*, 26 July 1969, p.1.

9. *First Annual Report to the Congress on the United States Foreign Policy for the 1970's*. 18 February 1970.

10. "Text of President's Message to Congress on Federal Budget for Fiscal Year 1971," *New York Times*, 3 February 1970, p.25.

11. Laird wrote President Nixon in late May to inform him that the state of the economy would soon force the administration to undertake greater reductions in the defense establishment than had been contemplated during the policy studies of 1969. President Nixon then turned the matter over for consideration to the National Security Council and Defense Program Review Committee (DPRC). NARA, Nixon Presidential Materials, NSC Institutional ("H") Files, NSC Meetings, Box H-029, Memorandum for the President, re: The Defense Budget, 31 May 1970 and Memorandum for the Secretary of Defense, 2 June 1970.

12. In the first volume of his memoirs, Henry Kissinger argued that by forcing the executive to concentrate on the "rearguard action to preserve a minimum arsenal," that, "Pentagon planners were forced to concentrate on preserving the existing force structure rather than adapting it to changed circumstances." This assertion, however, belies the fact that the administration had indeed considered rather far reaching reductions in the defense establishment. Henry Kissinger, *White House Years* (Boston: Little, Brown and Company, 1979), pp.212-15. These reviews included the DPRC Meeting, Defense Budget Review Session, 28 July 1970 at San Clemente and the NSC Meeting on the Defense Program, 19 August 1970. NARA, Nixon Presidential Materials, NSC Institutional ("H") Files, Box H-100 and Box H-29, respectively.

13. NARA, Nixon Presidential Materials, NSC Files, Subject Files, Box 319, Melvin Laird, *Strategy for Peace: A National Security Strategy of Realistic Deterrence,* Memorandum for the President from the Secretary of Defense, 6 November 1970. It was transmitted to the President under an EYES ONLY cover memorandum from Laird dated 7 November. The report itself is also available in DDRS, 2002, F178-179, 3043.

14. Laird was occasionally critical of McNamara's handling of the Pentagon, particular the method by which escalation in Vietnam took place, when serving on the Defense Subcommittee of the House Appropriations Committee in the mid-1960s. Trask and Goldberg, *The Department of Defense 1947-1997*, p.86, and Melvin R. Laird, "Iraq: Learning the Lessons of Vietnam," *Foreign Affairs* (November/December 2005).

15. Laird, *Strategy for Peace: A National Security Strategy of Realistic Deterrence*, p.59.

16. Ibid., p.60.

17. Ibid., p.52.

18. Ibid., p.61.

19. Ibid., p.62.

20. Laird had hoped his *Strategy for Peace: A National Security Strategy of Realistic Deterrence* would have been more closely integrated into the NSC and DPRC guidance for the Nixon administration's first Five-Year Defense program, but had been frustrated by the pace of events. Nonetheless, he incorporated broad features of it into his *Statement of Secretary of Defense Melvin R. Laird Before the House Armed Services Committee on the FY 1972-1976 Defense Program and the 1972 Defense Budget* of 9 March 1971. It also served as his tentative strategic guidance for the Department of Defense's programs and budgets. NARA, Nixon Presidential Materials, NSC Files, Subject File, Box 319, Memorandum for Dr. Kissinger, 5 February 1971.

21. There were occasionally calls in the military literature to heed Laird's recommendations. Colonel Sam Holliday argued that the US Army needed to look to a future where stabilization operations were accorded a mission status coequal

with planning for nuclear and conventional war. He urged the Army to develop two new organizations, Regional Assistance Commands (RAC), and Military Assistance (MA) Divisions. The RAC would "provide a pool of individuals and teams to support internal defense and development operations in a given region, and train leaders of that region in such activities." They would provide a focus within the Army for developing regional specialists, presumably with the language and cultural expertise that matched given requirements. The Regional Assistance Commands would be supported by the MA Division. The MA Division was not to be made up of a fixed number of brigades, but rather have the flexibility to absorb or detach several types of brigades as needed. These would include an advisory brigade, which provided local and team advisors to the host country; brigades to provide engineering, transportation, logistic, reconnaissance, and administrative specializations to the host countries forces; and light infantry and/or airmobile brigades to provide a sizable striking force to hit lager concentrations of guerilla forces. The point of deploying the MA Division would be to help stabilize situations before they deteriorated to the point that the US found itself facing the choice of major combat troop commitments such as in Vietnam. Sam C. Holliday, "Future Forces for the Army," *Military Review*, v.L, n.12 (December 1970), pp.86-92. See also Andrew J. Bacevich, Jr., "A Dissenting View of the Next War," *Armor*, v.LXXXV, n.5 (September-October 1976), pp.41-43, and Donald B. Vought, "Preparing for the Wrong War?," *Military Review*, v.LVII, n.9 (September 1977), pp.16-34. The issue has also recently resurfaced in the context of the Army's continuing transformation. See the comments by Lieutenant General Peter Chiarelli in "Learning from Our Modern War," *Military Review*, v.LXXXVII, n.5 (September-October 2007), pp.7-8.

22. Quoted in Trask and Goldberg, *The Department of Defense 1947-1997*, p.86.

23. Trask and Goldberg, *The Department of Defense 1947-1997*, pp.86-89.

24. Schlesinger in turn was replaced by Donald Rumsfeld, who had served as Ford's Chief of Staff and previously as US Ambassador to NATO. On Rumsfeld's tenure as Secretary of Defense in the Ford administration, see Trask and Goldberg, *The Department of Defense 1947-1997*, pp.94-95; James Mann, *Rise of the Vulcans: The History of Bush's War Cabinet* (New York: Viking, 2004), pp.65-78; and Rowan Scarborough, *Rumsfeld's War: The Untold Story of America's Anti-Terrorist Commander* (Washington, DC: Regnery Publishing, 2004), pp.79-84.

25. Trask and Goldberg, *The Department of Defense 1947-1997*, pp.90-93.

26. Birtle, *U.S. Army Counterinsurgency and Counterinsurgency Operations Doctrine 1942-1976*, p.479.

27. Ibid., pp.480-81.

28. There had been a dedicated course on Internal Defense and Development Operations since 1961-62 that was eliminated by 1973-74. Ball, *On Responsible Command*, rev. edn., p.423.

70

29. A nonbinding resolution calling for unilateral US troop reductions in NATO Europe was first introduced by Democratic Congressman Mike Mansfield in August 1966. Thomas A. Schwartz, *Lyndon Johnson and Europe: In the Shadow of Vietnam* (Cambridge, MA: Harvard University Press, 2003), pp.121-22, and Phil Williams, *The Senate and US Troops in Europe* (New York: St. Martin's Press, 1985), pp.143-55.

30. John S. Duffield, *Power Rules: The Evolution of NATO's Conventional Force Posture*, (Stanford, CA: Stanford University Press, 1995), p.196.

31. Kissinger surveys some of the domestic pressure in *White House Years*, pp.199-202. Senator J .William Fulbright, for instance, published *The Pentagon Propaganda Machine* (New York: Random House, 1970 and Vintage, 1971) which claimed the Pentagon presented inflated estimates of the Soviet threat to win appropriations. On economic problems and Nixon's response to them, see Diane B. Kunz, *Butter and Guns: America's Cold War Economic Diplomacy* (New York: The Free Press, 1997), pp.193-222.

32. Nixon Library (Online), National Security Decision Memoranda [hereafter NSDM] 88: US Force Levels in Europe and "Burden-Sharing," 15 October 1970. Available online at: http://www.nixonlibrary.gov/virtuallibrary/documents/nationalsecuritymemoranda.php.

33. In a report to Henry Kissinger, Martin Hillenbrand wrote that: "'Burden sharing' has three aspects: (1) the Europeans doing more for their and NATO defenses (improvements in conventional forces, ets.); (2) the US encouraging such efforts by upholding and improving its own conventional capabilities; (3) the Europeans assisting the US to offset its foreign exchange costs entailed in maintaining troops abroad (so-called 'offset')." NARA, Nixon Presidential Materials, NSC Institutional ("H") Files, National Security Study Memorandums, Box H-128, Report on US Policy Toward NATO under a cover memorandum dated 27 March 1969, p.8.

34. NSDM 95: U.S. Strategy and Forces for NATO, 25 November 1970, Nixon Library. Available at http://www.nixonlibrary.gov/virtuallibrary/documents/nationalsecuritymemoranda.php.

35. NSDM 95: U.S. Strategy and Forces for NATO.

36. "Reserve, Guard Get Buildup Role," *The Washington Post*, 9 September 1970, p.1.

37. Stewart, gen. ed., *American Military History*, v.II, p.385.

38. Chapman, *The Origins and Development of the National Training Center*, pp.33-37.

39. This account of Army reorganization is based on James A. Bowden, *Operation STEADFAST: The United States Army Reorganizes Itself* (US Marine Corps Command and Staff College, April 1985). Available online at: http://www.globalsecurity.org/military/library/report/1985/BJA.htm. The name STEADFAST originated with a reorganization plan developed at CONARC, in part to counter

the reorganization plans that DePuy and Kalergis were developing. Curiously, the official TRADOC history of this period does not discuss these antecedents to Operation STEADFAST, instead taking up the narrative under General Creighton Abrams when STEADFAST was put into operation. Anne W. Chapman, et. al., *Prepare the Army for War: A Historical Overview of the Army Training and Doctrine Command 1973-1988* (Fort Monroe, VA: Military History Office, TRADOC, 1998), p.7.

40. Lewis Sorley, *Thunderbolt: General Creighton Abrams and the Army of His Times* (New York: Simon and Schuster, 1992), p.342.

41. Ibid., p.346.

42. Ibid., pp.335, 349. The "Tooth-toTail" issue is one of long-standing and ongoing interest. For a recent overview, see John J. McGrath, *The Other End of the Spear: The Tooth-to-Tail Ratio (T3R) in Modern Military Operations* (Fort Leavenworth, KS: Combat Studies Institute, 2007).

43. *Department of the Army Historical Summary: FY 1973*, p.44. Available online at: http://www.army.mil/cmh/html/bookshelves/collect/Department of the Army Historical Summary.html. Also Fred Hoffman, "Reorganization Set by Army," *The Washington Post*, 11 January 1973, p.A2.

44. *Department of the Army Historical Summary: FY 1973*, pp.44-46.

45. Sorley, *Thunderbolt*, pp.364-65.

46. Comments by General Fred C. Weyand, Creighton Abrams' successor as Army Chief of Staff, quoted in Harry G. Summers, Jr., *On Strategy II: A Critical Analysis of the Gulf War* (New York: Dell Publishing, 1992), pp.74-75.

47. For a careful analysis of these factors, see Lock-Pullan, *US Army Intervention Policy and Army Innovation*, pp.51-53.

48. Nixon had indicated at a press conference in January that he intended to move relations with European allies to the front burner in 1973. During the early months of 1973, however, President Nixon himself was increasingly preoccupied with the developing revelations that led to the Watergate Scandal. Kissinger, at Nixon's direction, attempted to restart the "Year of Europe" project with a speech to the Associated Press editors in New York in mid-April. Kissinger's speech piqued the West Europeans as much as anything. Robert Dallek has argued that the "Year of Europe" was based on little of substance, and was primarily "a major part of Nixon's second-term PR campaign." Dallek, *Nixon and Kissinger*, p.466.

49. Conrad C. Crane, *Avoiding Vietnam: The US Army's Response to Defeat in Southeast Asia* (Carlisle, PA: Strategic Studies Institute, Army War College, September 2002), pp.3-6; Lock-Pullan, *US Army Intervention Policy and Army Innovation*, pp.53-56.

50. The Astarita Report cited here is a version written by then Lieutenant Colonel Harry G. Summers, Jr., a member of the Strategic Assessment Group, in 1974 as an Occasional Paper for the Strategic Studies Institute, which was then reprinted by direction of Vice Chief of Staff General John Vessey, Jr., in 1981. DTIC

accession number A098700. See also Sorley, *Thunderbolt*, pp.346-47.

51. Astarita Report, p.21.

52. Ibid., p.23.

53. Ibid., p.36.

54. Ibid., p.38.

55. This became a persistent theme of the generation of officers who served in Vietnam, and found its clearest expression in the Weinberger and Powell Doctrines. For a fascinating view of the long-term institutional roots of this problem, see Robert M. Cassidy, "Prophets or Praetorians? The Uptonian Paradox and the Powell Corollary," *Parameters*, v.XXXIII (Autumn 2003), pp.130-43.

56. Ibid., p.44.

57. General Fred C. Weyand had served as Vice Chief of Staff under Abrams when the Strategic Assessment Group was formed and then as Chief of Staff from 1974-1976. Fred C. Weyand and Harry G. Summers, Jr., "Serving the People: The Need for Military Power," *Military Review*, v.LVI, n.12 (December 1976), pp.8-18.

58. General DePuy stressed this point in a letter to General Weyand on 18 February 1976. It is reprinted in Romjue, *From Active Defense to AirLand Battle*, pp.82-86.

59. The problem being that there was little confidence in NATO that the West's conventional forces were strong enough to prolong the conventional battle for more than a few days, though there was some range of opinion on this matter. The British Army of the Rhine (BAOR), which was responsible for the northern portions of the central front in West Germany, had been judged to be capable of holding out for as little as two days in SACUER's Current Conventional Capability Appraisal (known as the Mountbatten Study in the mid-1960s. In any case, the BAOR and many of the other European NATO allies did not maintain sufficient conventional stocks of ammunition and fuel for prolonged conventional combat. This note is drawn from the author's forthcoming dissertation, "The Dilemma of NATO Strategy, 1949-1968" (PhD dissertation, Ohio University, 2008), chap.7. My information on the Mountbatten Study comes from the British National Archives, DEFE 5/160, COS 133/65.

60. Sheehan, "Preparing for an imaginary war?," p.170.

61. US Army Combined Arms Center, *Analysis of Combat Data-1973 War*, 9 vols. (July 1974).

62. See "Implications of the Middle East War on U.S. Army Tactics" in Swain, ed., *Selected Papers of General William E. DePuy*, pp.75-112.

63. Ibid., p.76.

64. Sorley, *Thunderbolt*, pp.372-78.

65. DePuy's contribution to the Army's "doctrinal revolution" has been well treated in: Paul H. Herbert, "Deciding What Has to Be Done: General William E. DePuy and the 1976 Edition of FM 100-5," *Leavenworth Papers*, n.16 (Fort

Leavenworth, KS: Combat Studies Institute, 1988); John L. Romjue, *From Active Defense to AirLand Battle: The Development of Army Doctrine 1973-1982* (Fort Monroe, VA: TRADOC, 1984), pp.3-14; Roger J. Spiller, "In the Shadow of the Dragon: Doctrine and the US Army after Vietnam," *RUSI Journal*, v.142, n.6 (December 1997), pp.41-54; and Richard M. Swain, ed., *Papers of General William E. DePuy* (Fort Leavenworth, KS: Combat Studies Institute, 1994).

66. General DePuy to General Weyand, 18 February 1976. Reprinted in Romjue, *From Active Defense to AirLand Battle*, p.83.

67. Citino, *Blitzkrieg to Desert Storm*, pp.256-62, and Romjue, *From Active Defense to AirLand Battle*, pp.13ff.

68. FM 100-5 (1976 edition), p.1-4.

69. Chapman, *The Origins and Development of the National Training Center*, pp.7-8.

70. Indeed, this had been a problem of long-standing for the armor community. Lieutenant Colonel Albin R. Irzyk wrote in 1954 about the Armor School at Fort Knox that "training areas have long been too limited for other than small-unit problems." See Irzyk, "Revolution in Armor Education," *Armor*, v.LXIII, n.4 (July-August 1954), p.42.

71. Chapman, *The Origins and Development of the National Training Center*, pp.14-15.

72. To provide realistic training at the NTC, an Opposing Force was created. In 1976 the Assistant CSA, Intelligence, had arranged Department of Defense and Department of State support to train a group of soldiers in Soviet weapons and tactics. TRADOC produced a number of manuals to support the Opposing Force. FM 30-102 OPFOR Europe, completed in 1978, was the first fruit of this new project. See *Department of the Army Historical Summary: FY 1978*, p.27. The study of Warsaw Pact doctrine and training also received attention at Fort Leavenworth, where the Soviet Army Studies Office (SASO) was established. The prolific historian of the Soviet military, David M. Glantz, was one of the primary contributors to the SASO effort. Citino, *Blitzkrieg to Desert Storm*, p.261.

73. Chapman, *The Origins and Development of the National Training Center*, p.41.

74. Ibid., pp.85-86.

75. Ibid., p.47.

76. Ibid., pp.68-69.

77. Vetock, *Lessons Learned*, p. 125.

78. Edward M. Coffman, "The Course of Military History in the United States Since World War II," *The Journal of Military History*, v.61, n.4 (October 1997), p.770.

79. Ibid., pp.770-71.

80. Brooks E. Kleber, "The Army Looks At Its Need for Military History," *Military Affairs*, v.37, n.2 (April 1973), pp.47-48.

81. Ibid.

82. Coffman, "The Course of Military History in the United States Since World War II," p.771.

83. Ball, *Of Responsible Command*, rev. edn., p.410.

84. Ibid., pp.392-96.

85. Dastrup, *The US Army Command and General Staff College*, p.120.

86. Ibid., pp.121-22.

87. *A Review of the Education and Training for Officers* [hereafter *RETO*] (Washington, DC: Headquarters, Department of the Army, 30 June 1978), v.1, p.I-2. *RETO* was a 5 volume study. Volume 1, which contains the executive summary, is available on DTIC, accession # ADA070772, at: http://handle.dtic.mil/100.2/ADA070772.

88. *RETO*, v.1, p.v.

89. *Department of the Army Historical Summary: FY 1980*, p.44.

90. *RETO*, v.1, p.XI-5.

91. *RETO*, v.1, p.E-4-15.

92. *Department of the Army Historical Summary: FY 1980*, p.44.

93. My thanks to Kelvin Crow, Assistant CAC Command Historian, for providing me access to the CAC Historian's Working Files regarding the establishment of the Combat Studies Institute. For Generals Starry and Thurman's interest in Dupuy's book and the *Kriegakademie*, see Memorandum for the Record, re: Establishment of a Combat Studies Research and Analysis Activity at Fort Leavenworth, 5 September 1978 and Minutes of Faculty Council Meeting, 14 September 1978. Trevor N. Dupuy, *A Genius for War: The German Army General Staff, 1807-1945* (Englewood Cliffs, NJ: Prentice-Hall, 1977).

94. For the best account of CSI origins, see Roger J. Spiller, "War History and the History Wars: Establishing the Combat Studies Institute," *The Public Historian*, v.10, n.4 (Fall 1998), pp.65-81.

95. An undated draft letter from the fall of 1978 from Lieutenant General Thurman stated: "The Combat Studies Institute (CSI), Command and General Staff College, conducts interpretive, analytical studies on combat and combat-related subjects, and teaches part of the curriculum of the USACGSC. As such, the mission of CSI includes both research and teaching." CAC Historian's Working Files, Folder: Formative Documents of CSI, Letter of Instruction on Combat Studies Institute, Command and General Staff College, undated. See also Dastrup, *The US Army Command and General Staff College*, p.122.

96. Ball, *Of Responsible Command*, rev. edn., p.452. For a critical view of this course, see John M. Collins, "Vietnam Postmortem: A Senseless Strategy," *Parameters*, v.VIII, n.1 (March 1978), p.13.

97. Ibid.

98. Richard Duncan Downie, *Learning From Conflict: The U.S. Military in Vietnam, El Salvador, and the Drug War* (Westport, CT: Praeger, 1998), pp.70-74.

99. BDM Corporation, *A Study of Strategic Lessons Learned in Vietnam*, 8 vols. (1979-80). Abstracts and some full texts of these volumes are available on-line at the Defense Technical Information Centers website: http://www.dtic.mil/.

100. Harry G. Summers, Jr. *On Strategy: The Vietnam War in Context* (Carlisle Barracks, PA: Strategic Studies Institute, 1981), and *On Strategy: A Critical Analysis of the Vietnam War* (Novato, CA: Presidio Books, 1982). It was reprinted in a paperback edition by Dell in 1984 and 1995. It is currently listed on the Army Chief of Staff's Reading List at the Combined Arms Research Library, and as recommended reading in Stewart, gen. ed., *American Military History*, vol.II, p.368.

101. Summers, *On Strategy: A Critical Assessment of the Vietnam War*, p.27.

102. Cassidy, "Prophets or Praetorians?," pp.138-39; Downie, *Learning from Conflict*, pp.73-74; and Lock-Pullan, *US Army Intervention Policy and Army Innovation*, pp.119-20.

103. Some notable military intellectuals were in fact trying to focus Army attention on strategy for more likely contingencies, but the criticisms of existing strategy they developed did not resonate very well with Summers' argument. For examples, see Robert Leider, "An Old Strategist Speaks to the Young," *Military Review*, v.LIV, n.2 (February 1974), pp.3-15; Andrew J. Bacevich, Jr., "Dissenting View of the Next War," *Armor*, v.LXXXV, n.5 (Sept.-Oct. 1976), pp.41-43; Donald B. Vought, "Preparing for the Wrong War?," *Military Review*, v.LVII, n.9 (September 1977), pp.16-34; John M. Collins, "Vietnam Postmortem: A Senseless Strategy," *Parameters*, v.VIII, n.1 (March 1978), pp.8-14; and William O. Staudenmaier, "Military Strategy in Transition," *Parameters*, v.VIII, n.4 (December 1978), pp.28-36.

104. Cassidy, "Prophets or Praetorians?," p.139; and Lock-Pullan, *US Army Intervention Policy and Army Innovation*, pp.120-22.

105. The body had undergone a number of name changes. These included Advanced Studies Group; the Doctrine and Studies Group; and the Institute for Advanced Studies. It had been transferred under the Combat Developments Command in the reorganization of 1962, though it remained located at the War College. See Ball, *Of Responsible Command*, rev. edn., p.357, and Hewes, *From Root to McNamara*, p.360.

106. Ball, *Of Responsible Command*, rev. edn., p.421.

107. Ibid., pp.424-25.

108. A search of the Combined Arms Research Library at Fort Leavenworth returned nearly 20 titles for the Strategic Studies Institute, Art of War Colloquium for 1983. They included titles such as: *Count Schlieffen and the World War*; *The development of Strategic Science during the 19th Century*; *Generalship in the World War: Comparative Studies*; *Principles of War: The American Genesis*; *Selected German Operations on the Eastern Front*; *The Soviet Battlefield Development Plan*; and *Soviet Operational Concepts*.

109. Hawkins and Carafano, *Prelude to Army XXI*, p.19.

110. "An Assessment of the Conventional Warfighting Capability of the US Army in Central Europe" by Lieutenant General James F. Hollingsworth, 30 June 1976, DDRS, 1998, F175-176, 1936. Unfortunately this author has not yet seen the full report. Also "US Reassessing Strategy in Europe," *New York Times*, 24 September 1976, p.7. One important caveat should be noted, which is that the US and its NATO allies consistently failed to undertake a force buildup to meet a full-scale Warsaw Pact attack through a purely conventional defense. The subject is well treated in Duffield, *Power Rules*, passim.

111. John L. Romjue, *The Army of Excellence: The Development of the 1980s Army* (Fort Monroe, VA: Office of the Command Historian, United States Army Training and Doctrine Command, 1993), pp.7-15.

112. It is unclear to this author in what ways the ROAD division could not have been so adapted, as was supposed to allow flexible assignment of battalions to brigades in any mix to suit the situation. Hence, if one wanted a "heavier" ROAD division one could either increase the ratio of armor battalions to infantry/mechanized battalions, or simply increase the number of battalions altogether, since in the ROAD structure each brigade could have up to five battalions assigned.

113. Hawkins and Carafano, *Prelude to Army XXI*, p.20. See also John W. Foss and Donald S. Phil, "The Division Restructuring Study," *Military Review*, v.LVII, n.3 (March 1977), pp.11-21.

114. *Department of the Army Historical Summary: FY 1978*, p.21, and Hawkins and Carafano, *Prelude to Army XXI*, pp.19-21.

115. Hawkins and Carafano, *Prelude to Army XXI*, p.24.

116. Ball, *Of Responsible Command*, rev. edn., p.462.

117. Romjue, *From Active Defense to AirLand Battle*, p.30.

118. For Roger Spiller, "by the time Starry's AirLand Battle doctrine was published, the doctrinal revolution was over. That revolution consisted not of the substance of the doctrine, but of the unprecedented functions doctrine had been made to serve and the way in which it had been given life." Spiller, "In the Shadow of the Dragon: Doctrine and the US Army after Vietnam," p.52.

119. Huba Wass de Czege and L. D. Holder, "The New FM 100-5," *Military Review*, v.LXII, n.7 (July 1982), pp.53-70.

120. FM 100-5 (1982), p.1-1.

121. Donn A. Starry, "Extending the Battlefield," *Military Review*, v.LXI, n.3 (March 1981), pp.31-50.

122. Ibid., p.32.

123. Ibid., p.34. In the early 1960s, Secretary of Defense McNamara had carefully scrutinized the need for tactical nuclear weapons in Europe. On the initiation of these studies, see *FRUS 1961-1963*, v.VIII, Doc 86: Memorandum from SecDef to CJCS, 23 May 1962, re: A Study of Tactical Nuclear Weapons and Continuation of the Study of Requirements for General Purpose Forces, and Doc.87:

Memorandum from the President's Military Representative, 25 May 1962, re: Study of the Requirements for Tactical Atomic Weapons, pp.294-300. For a declassified version of the initial study (with excisions), see DOD FOIA website, folder: Nuclear, Chemical, and Biological Matters, #362, Project 23: "Requirements for Tactical Nuclear Weapons," available at: http://www.dod.mil/pubs/foi/ncb/. Despite numerous studies, it was never clear that a legitimate warfighting role for tactical (or battlefield) weapons could be determined which would not escalate into general nuclear war. Towards the end of his tenure as Secretary of Defense, Robert McNamara wrote: "while the deterrent value of our theater nuclear capabilities is high, there are great uncertainties concerning the actual conduct and results of limited nuclear war." Memorandum for the President (draft), NATO Strategy and Force Structure, 16 January 1968. Similarly the following year, Clark Clifford, who was McNamara's successor as Secretary of Defense, wrote to President Johnson that "The NATO Defense Ministers in the Nuclear Planning Group have acknowledged that the number of [nuclear] weapons in Europe is adequate. In addition, they are uncertain as to how large numbers of these weapons could be used, except in general nuclear war." Memorandum for the President (draft), NATO Strategy and Force Structure, 7 January 1969. Both documents are available at the DOD FOIA website, folder: North Atlantic Treaty Organization, #331 and 332, http://www.dod.mil/pubs/foi/nato/. Looking back a decade after McNamara's attempt to grapple with the tactical nuclear weapon problem, SACEUR General Andrew Goodpaster would tell President Nixon that, "the issue of tactical nuclear weapons had now been stagnant for 10 years." NARA, Nixon Presidential Materials, National Security Council, Name Files, Box 816, Memo for Record, Nixon-Goodpaster Conversation, 15 February 1973.

124. For one of the best studies of NATO debates over strategy and nuclear weapons in the 1970s and 80s, see Ivo H. Daalder, *The Nature and Practice of Flexible Response: NATO Strategy and Theater Nuclear Forces Since 1967* (New York: Columbia University Press, 1991).

125. Dastrup, *The US Army Command and General Staff College*, pp.124-25.

126. Rose, *The Evolution of U.S. Army Nuclear Doctrine, 1945-1980*, p.xiii.

127. FM 101-31-1, *Staff Officers Field Manual-Nuclear Weapons Employment Doctrine and Procedures*, 6 January 1986.

128. Indeed, most of the articles in *Military Review* and *Parameters* on theater nuclear weapons were published in 1980-82, in the midst of the Euromissile debate. For instance: William D. Brown, "Whatever Happened to Tactical Nuclear Warfare?," *Military Review*, v.LX, n.1 (January 1980), pp.46-53; Philip W. Dyer, "The Moral Dimension of Tactical Nuclear Weapons in Europe," *Parameters*, v.X (June 1980), pp.44-50; Andrew E. Andrews, "Toward a Tactical Nuclear Doctrine," *Military Review*, v.LX, n.10 (October 1980), pp.13-19; John Borawski, "East-West Bargaining on Theater Nuclear Forces," *Parameters*, v.XI (1981), pp.31-38; Richard Brandt and Thomas Nagel, "The Morality of Tactical Nuclear

Weapons: A Philosophers' Debate," *Parameters*, v.XI (September 1981), pp.75-86; William R. McKinney, "Tactical Nuclear Weapons: The Practical Side," *Military Review*, v.LXI, n.10 (October 1981), pp.60-65; and Joseph D. Douglas, Jr., "The Theater Nuclear Threat," *Parameters*, v.XII (December 1982), pp.71-81.

129. Samuel F. Wells, Jr., "Reagan, Euromissiles, and Europe," in *The Reagan Presidency: Pragmatic Conservatism and Its Legacies*, ed. by W. Eliot Brownlee and Hugh Davis Graham (Lawrence, KS: University Press of Kansas, 2003), p.145.

130. Anticipating future force reductions, Army Chief of Staff Carl Vuono initiated the Anteus Study in the fall of 1987. Its purpose was to anticipate the force reductions which might develop from conventional arms limitations talks with the Soviets. The Anteus Study is discussed at further length in the following chapter.

131. See the discussion of the 1993 edition of FM 100-5 in the next chapter.

132. CAC History Office, *U.S. Army Combined Arms Center 1985 Annual Historical Review* (Fort Leavenworth, KS: US Army Combined Arms Center, 1986), pp.43-48. For Colonel Wass de Czege's recommendations for a second year course on the operational art of war, see Huba Wass de Czege, *Final Report, Army Staff College Level Training Study*, 13 June 1983, DTIC accession # ADA144852. Available at: http://handle.dtic.mil/100.2/ADA144852. Unfortunately Dastrup's *The US Army Command and General Staff College* was published before the founding of SAMS. At the time of this writing, Colonel (ret.) Kevin Benson is preparing a monograph on the adoption of operational art by the US Army as a doctoral dissertation at the University of Kansas. See also Chapman, et. al., *Prepare the Army for War*, pp.14-15; and L. D. Holder, "Education and Training for Theater Warfare," *Military Review*, v.LXX, n.9 (September 1990), pp.85-89.

133. Colonel Wass de Czege reported that the hours devoted to tactical instruction had dropped from "665 hours in 1951, to 582 hours in 1957, to 335 hours in 1968 and finally in 1974, to the recent level of 170 hours." *Final Report, Army Staff College Level Training Study*, p.37. The SSI study's full title was "Operation Planning: An Analysis of the Education and Development of Effective Army Planners." Major General Meloy had been dispatched to Fort Leavenworth to conduct a brief review of the CGSC curriculum by CSA General Edward Meyer in January 1982. Colonel Wass De Czege summarizes the conclusions of both reports in the appendix to his *Final Report, Army Staff College Level Training Study*.

134. Wass de Czege, *Final Report, Army Staff College Level Training Study*, p.10.

135. CAC History Office, *U.S. Army Combined Arms Center 1985 Annual Historical Review*, p.43; and Stewart, *American Military History*, vol.II, p.390.

136. Future CSA General Gordon Sullivan alluded to SAMS in 1990, stating that, "The army today is developing leaders and staff officers who are much more capable than their predecessors of translating strategic objectives into operational

plans and operational plans into tactical fire and maneuver." Gordon Sullivan, "Doctrine: An Army Update," in Robert L. Pfaltzgraff, Jr., and Richard H. Shultz, Jr., *The United States Army: Challenges and Missions for the 1990s* (Lexington, MA: Lexington Books, 1991), p.80. On the role of SAMS planners in the first Gulf War, see the favorable view in H. Norman Schwarzkopf, *It Doesn't Take a Hero* (New York: Linda Grey Bantam Books, 1992), pp.354-59.

Chapter 3
A Strange New World–The Army
after the Cold War

During the 1990s the Army tried to adapt to changes in mission while undergoing a considerable reduction in force structure. Defining this new environment and figuring out what needed to be done proved extremely difficult. Military analyst Edwin Luttwak, commenting on a wide-shared concern, argued in the mid-1990s that the Cold War's legacy, remained firmly embedded in a generation of officers and defense officials who were educated in the strategic culture of the Cold War. In particular, this meant that deterrence was seen as the primary role of military force. One consequence of this was a reluctance to use military force unless "vital" interests were at stake, a precondition which became essentially a prohibition.[1] The loss of American forces in Somalia in October 1993 only heightened this proscription for some, and contributed to the long-running wrangle over whether or not US forces could and should be used in the Balkans. When US forces were eventually introduced into the region, it led General Wesley Clark, who served at SACEUR during the NATO intervention in Bosnia and during the short-lived air campaign against Serbia, to posit that a new type of modern war, always essentially limited in its nature, was emerging.[2] Given the unhappy past experience of the US military in "limited" wars like Korea and Vietnam, this seemed to portend another era of difficult civil-military relations and more generally, an uneasiness over the future of American grand strategy.

Determining the utility of military force was a central debate in US foreign and defense policy in the 1990s. The question of the utility of military force in turn had profound implications for the roles and missions that the Army would be called upon to perform. Recent scholarship on the period has a decidedly critical ring to it. Richard Lock-Pullan has argued that post-Cold War adaptation "was hampered by the time it took for its agents of policy to adapt to the new environment, and to develop a new and appropriate identity." The hope of "assertive multilateralism" was quickly dashed by the mission-creep of the Somalian venture, making change "too fast for the Army to adapt in time; the era began just as sufficient learning had taken place to address the strategic requirements of the previous strategic environment."[3] Historian Brian Linn in a recent study of the "Army's way of war," has argued that "in the decade after the Gulf War, neither the army leadership nor the institutions charged with preparing for the next war could refocus from the Cold War's epic Soviet-American clash. What had been billed in the 1970s and early 1980s as a doctrinal revolution congealed into intellectual inertia and institutional complacency."[4] Though sweeping judgments about the 1990s are difficult, this chapter will review the attempts by the US Army to adapt itself to the post-Cold War, post-Gulf War world.[5]

Reductions in Cold War tensions in the late 1980s, and especially the revolutionary events of 1989-91, indicated to many contemporary observers that the Cold War was winding down and a new security environment was to emerge. The process of defining strategic priorities proved elusive for both the Army, and more basically, the country as a whole, for much of the decade following the end of the Cold War.[6] This latest round of downsizing and reduced budgets, coupled with the changed strategic environment, caused considerable consternation in the US defense establishment. This problem was exacerbated by tense civil-military relations during the Clinton presidency. The reductions affected the Army especially, and by the late 1990s the active force was at its smallest size since 1939.[7] In addition to defense reductions, the passage of the Goldwater-Nichols Act in 1986 had important implications for the US military during the 1990s which are also considered. Congress played an increasingly assertive role throughout the 1990s, pressing the Defense Department to conduct the Commission on Roles and Missions of the Armed Services in 1994-95, then instituting a Quadrennial Defense Review from 1997 on. The US Army fastened onto the Force XXI modernization program beginning in 1994, which was "defined as the process of building an army for the twenty-first century."[8] However, this modernization and adaptation campaign was not necessarily successful in solving problems revolving around roles and missions. These questions have in practice been largely answered in the immediate term only by the prolonged nature of the global war on terror. One strongly suspects that they will soon have to be addressed again.

Like the earlier eras surveyed, the US military in the 1990s had to face the prospect of leaner times ahead. Starting under the administration of George H. W. Bush and accelerating into the Clinton presidency, the US government sought to reap a "peace dividend" from the end of the Cold War.[9] At the same time, bereft of "enemy number one," the US military found itself increasingly called upon to justify itself in terms of its intervention and humanitarian capabilities. Difficult deployments in Somalia, Haiti, the Balkans, and elsewhere presented challenges to the Army as an institution which for 45-plus years had used the Soviet challenge as its central mission focus.

The successful outcome of the Gulf War in some ways complicated the adaptation picture. It was perceived as validating the Army's AirLand Battle doctrine and the training methodologies which had been developed since the Vietnam War.[10] As the political scientist Richard Lock-Pullan has written, "the Gulf War vindicated the lessons the Army had learnt from the Vietnam War," but the lessons were the ones the Army wanted to learn.[11] At the same time, it was seen as a watershed between two eras, in the sense that it seemed to signal the end to the era in which preparation for fighting a war against a large-scale Soviet-style opponent should be the Army's primary focus. Indeed, the 1990s Army was increasingly called upon to support military interventions that were more focused on peace-keeping and supporting the UN.[12] The more traditional role of serving as a deterrent to major war receded into the background after the end of the Cold War. This created questions as to how the Army should deal with these challenges. In part, the Army responded by using its institutionalized mechanisms for adaptation. For instance, TRADOC issued a revised FM 100-5 in 1993. A second revision was underway in the middle of the decade, only to be put on hold as Army doctrine was coordinated with the new wave of Joint Doctrine being produced. Ultimately the 1993 edition of FM 100-5 was replaced in 2001 with FM 3-0 Operations. But the vagaries of setting out a fixed doctrine in an unsettled strategic environment made reliance on DePuy's formula for change less-than-entirely satisfactory. General Gordon Sullivan, Chief of Staff of the Army from 1991-95, attempted to initiate a new process of adaptive learning with the so-called new Louisiana Maneuvers. Sullivan's idea for a new process for change never completely caught on, however, and eventually a series of programs for modernization/transformation—Force XXI, Army After Next, and Army Transformation—followed one another in short order.[13]

The Impact of the Goldwater-Nichols Act

The Goldwater-Nichols Act (Public Law 99-433), signed into law on 1 October 1986, was the culmination of the long-running debate over organization, planning, acquisition, and management of the Department of Defense that stretched back to the Vietnam era. It was the first major legislative change to the Department of Defense since the DOD Reorganization Act of 1958.[14] Goldwater-Nichols aimed to improve military advice given to the President by increasing the authority of the Chief of Staff vis-à-vis the individual service chiefs and creating a new position of Vice Chief of Staff as the second highest ranking military official in the armed forces. The Act also strengthened the position of the unified and specified commanders by placing them directly in the operational chain of command running from the President to the Secretary of Defense to the unified or specified commander. The commanders were also given enhanced authority over all component activities within their bailiwick.[15] The Act also placed considerable stress on cultivating officers with a strong joint background, stipulating that at least half the officers in joint duty positions be nominated and qualified for joint specialty designation. This required attendance of a joint professional military school, which at the time the Act was passed included only the Armed Forces Staff College and two components of the National Defense University.[16] Finally, the Act also stipulated that the President transmit annually to Congress a National Security Strategy Report at the same time the budget request was submitted. It was to outline vital national interests and delineate the capabilities the US had to carry out its national security strategy.[17] Secretary of Defense Robert Gates has recently commented that, "Getting the military services to work together was a recurring battle that had to be addressed time and again, and was only really resolved" by the passage and implementation of Goldwater-Nichols.[18]

The Army of the 1990s

Progress towards arms control, important shifts in the Soviet Union's domestic policies (Gorbachev's glasnost and perestroika), and the rising costs of the early Reagan era defense buildup led to increasing US domestic criticism over the costs of defense in the later 1980s. As early as the fall of 1987, Army Chief of Staff General Carl Vuono authorized the Anteus Study to review the Army's force structure, especially in Europe, in light of these factors. The Anteus Study was completed by October 1989. It envisioned reductions in Army forces over the coming decade from 771,000 active duty soldiers and 18 divisions to a force of 640,000 active duty soldiers and 15 divisions.[19] However, Congressional and domestic pressure for a Cold War peace dividend grew apace with the dramatic changes in Eastern Europe. In the fall of 1989, Chairman of the Joint Chiefs General Colin Powell began developing a concept for a Base Force.[20] According to General Powell, he had first contemplated a 500,000 man "Base Force" Army as part of one of Lieutenant General William DePuy's ad hoc study groups nearly twenty years earlier.[21] Despite opposition from the Chiefs, who opposed cuts of the magnitude proposed in the Base Force, Powell earned President Bush's approval for the concept on 1 August. The Base Force became the administration's official position for minimum future defense levels. It called for reductions in active duty end strength from 2.1 million to 1.6 million, with an active duty Army of 535,000 men and 12 divisions.[22]

84

On 2 August 1990 President Bush, accompanied by British Prime Minister Margaret Thatcher, delivered an address marking the 40th anniversary of the Aspen Institute in Colorado. In the midst of a budget fight in Congress over the defense budget, and with Iraq's invasion of Kuwait just hitting the newsstands, President Bush outlined the need for new defense capabilities in the new strategic environment. While not dismissing completely the need to be wary of Soviet capabilities, President Bush was hopeful about the possibilities to "seize the historic opportunity to create a lasting peace." Within two months, West and East Germany would be officially reunified under a plan that called for Soviet withdrawal and allowed the newly reunited Germany to remain a member of the North Atlantic Treaty Organization. President Bush emphasized that American interests in global stability would necessitate "maintaining a forward presence" in Europe (where US forces would remain "as long as we are wanted and needed"), the Pacific, the Mediterranean, and the Persian Gulf. Echoing a theme that would have been very familiar to an observer of the US military in the late 1950s or early 1960s, he called for, "A new emphasis on flexibility and versatility." This would be required to better project power from the continental United States rapidly overseas when called upon, which harkened back to the thrust of Eisenhower's New Look.[23] President Bush also wanted to avoid false economies in research and development, and retain a premium on training and readiness of the active force.[24] Reflecting Powell's Base Force plan, President Bush outlined a gradual reduction of defense spending by 25 percent over a five year period, but emphasized that he and his chief advisers did not simply want across the board reductions. Reflecting on the lessons of earlier rapid draw-downs and the very different reality of dealing with an all volunteer force, the Bush administration aimed for an orderly transition that would "not break faith with the young men and women who have freely chosen to serve their country."[25]

Commenting on the President's outline, Chief of Staff General Carl Vuono wrote that the Army needed power projection capabilities with a mix of rather traditional forces, including armored, light, and special operations forces, which could be "tailored into force packages to meet the specific challenge at hand." In addition to reduced forward forces abroad, the Army needed to be prepared to rely on only five active divisions in the continental US that could rapidly deploy and serve as the "building blocks" for future force packages. Given the need for power projection, General Vuono advocated "substantial improvement in our sealift and airlift as a matter of urgent national priority."[26] Reflecting his lack of support for the Base Force, General Vuono argued that the projected reductions would leave "a perilously small force" which would "entail acceptance of greater national risk as a consequence of our reduced capacity to resolve large-scale or simultaneous crises solely with active component forces."[27] Vuono's concern, however, was lost on the Bush administration, which faced Congressional pressure led in part by House Armed Service Chairman Les Aspin (D–WI) for even deeper cuts than those proposed in the Base Force. Though any administration elected in 1992 would have faced pressure for cuts in defense spending, President-elect Bill Clinton's selection of Aspin to serve as his first Secretary of Defense brought into the DOD one of the principal advocates for deeper cuts.[28] During the early Clinton years, the US military faced dramatic cuts in expenditures, cuts which fell especially hard on personnel, while the growing demand for contingency operations and interventions would place increasing strain on those who remained behind. Poor civil-military relations further exacerbated this era of transition. In the midst of these difficulties the Army continued its quest for appropriate doctrine and force structure to meet these new challenges.

Doctrinal Revision

In the spring of 1990, TRADOC Commander General John Foss and Chief of Staff General Vuono had begun discussing the next stage of Army doctrinal revision. Preliminarily they had decided to place emphasis on the operational level of planning for joint operations. Before this project advanced very far, TRADOC became pre-occupied with training forces, especially reservists, for deployment to the Persian Gulf.[29] After the Gulf War came to its quick conclusion, Colonel James McDonough, the director of SAMS, who was tasked with the doctrine rewrite, suggested that undue haste might be unproductive.[30] This probably reflected the need to first process the insights from the recently completed war. In addition, both the CSA and TRADOC commanders turned-over in the summer of 1991. The impact of two new commanders in such critical spots was bound to impact the direction of doctrinal revision.

General Vuono's successor as Chief of Staff was General Gordon R. Sullivan. Sullivan would preside over the Army's attempts to adapt to the challenges of the post-Cold War world. He had previously served as Vuono's Vice Chief of Staff, Assistant Commandant of the Armor School, Deputy Commandant at the Command and General Staff College, Commander of the 1st Infantry Division, and Deputy Chief of Staff for Operations and Plans. Sullivan's tours at the Armor School and CGSC had stimulated his interest in the potential of simulation-based training, and during his tour at Fort Riley as Commander of the 1st Infantry Division, he mused over the potential to combine live and virtual exercises to develop a modern version of the "Louisiana Maneuvers."[31]

Sullivan selected Lieutenant General Frederick M. Franks, Jr. to assume command of TRADOC. Lieutenant General Franks had previously served as Commander of VII Corps, overseeing the deployment, positioning, and maneuver of a powerful five division force during the Gulf War. He had past experience at TRADOC as a combat developments planning group chief under General Donn Starry, had served as an executive officer under both General Starry and General Glenn Otis, and had served as Deputy Commandant of CGSC from 1985-87. Before assuming command, Sullivan had informed Franks that he saw the TRADOC commander as a "catalyst" for leading the Army into the future. For Sullivan and Franks, TRADOC's production of a new operational doctrine would be one of the keys to the Army's development in the next generation.[32] In this sense, both men were products of the post-1973 TRADOC revolution that saw doctrine as a driving engine of Army change.[33]

Drafting of the new manual was primarily conducted at the School of Advanced Military Studies at Fort Leavenworth. This did not mean that the new doctrine was exclusively the purview of SAMS or even TRADOC. Sullivan and Franks cultivated and encouraged views from throughout the Army. To stimulate thinking about the new doctrine revision, teams from both SAMS and TRADOC conducted a number of briefings in the fall of 1991 to the Fall Army Commanders Conference (16-19 October), an Army-Air Force "4-Star Summit" (14-15 November), and at the Senior Leaders Warfighting Conference (20-21 November).[34] Colonel McDonough and others also published a number of articles in the leading Army journals to solicit views.[35] A number of issues arose in these discussions. These included the need to integrate a broader spectrum of conflict into Army doctrine, including operations short or war and post-conflict operations. With retrenchment on the horizon, issues of mobilization and logistics for power projection also loomed large. The success of the Gulf War's air campaign also stirred up old elements of controversy between the Army and Air Force. The need to assert the primacy of land power, and fights over the range of weapons system (echoing the 1950s) again intruded in discussions of proper Army doctrine.[36] Clearly the doctrine writers faced an imposing task in 1991-92 bringing together this broad range of issues.

General Franks distributed draft chapters on the Army in the strategic environment, operations short of war, and crisis response to the Army

Senior Leader's Conference in late March 1992. The choice of chapters generated some friction amongst the field commanders, who wanted to be sure the manual's primary focus remained on war fighting doctrine. This fitted well with General Franks' own approach. In early March he had informed his drafting team of the need to focus on the strategic-operational-tactical linkages. For Franks these were represented by five "battle dynamics," which were: 1) "early deployment, lethality, and survivability; 2) the notion of increased depth; 3) increased battle space; 4) command and control and tempo; and 5) combat service support." These "battle dynamics" would be central to the final manual.[37] This was a rather traditional focus on mid-to-high intensity conflict, and suggested that operations short of war and post-conflict operations were quickly becoming areas of peripheral concern in the new manual.

The new FM 100-5 was released in June 1993. Reflecting the outlook and conviction of the generation of officers whose views were shaped by the Vietnam War, the manual emphasized that the decision "to employ military forces exemplify the dynamic link among the people, the government, and the military." Critical to this link was the support of the American people, who, according to the manual:

> . . . expect decisive victory and abhor unnecessary casualties. They prefer quick resolution of conflicts and reserve the right to reconsider their support should any of these conditions not be met. They demand timely and accurate information on the conduct of military operations.[38]

The Army had to be able to conduct full-dimensional, joint operations which included "nation assistance, counterdrug operations, security assistance, deterrence, and stability operations" in addition to the ability to conduct sustained and decisive land combat.[39]

Even with the publication of the new FM 100-5 in June 1993, the role of doctrine in the 1990s was unclear. On the one hand, there was a considerable institutionalized doctrine-writing apparatus in the Army, a clear legacy of the creation of TRADOC and DePuy's doctrinal revolution. On the other hand, the fluidity of the international environment and the difficulties in determining the proper role for US armed forces was reflected in an ambiguity regarding doctrine. This ambiguity was reflected in TRADOC Pamphlet 525-5: Force XXI Operations released just a year after the new FM 100-5, which stated that, "for our Army's needs, doctrine in the present and predicted strategic environments will be much less prescriptive and much less given to precise, scientific analysis than military doctrine of the Cold War." Even more emphatically, it stated that "There can be no single, prescribed, authoritative Army doctrine for this strategic period."[40]

The New Louisiana Maneuvers

While the doctrinal revisions of FM 100-5 were underway, General Sullivan continued to pursue his interest in changing the Army's methodology of change. During the first few months of his tenure, his idea was still somewhat amorphous. But running throughout his thinking was the idea of developing something akin to the Louisiana Maneuvers of 1941. In October 1991, Sullivan read Christopher R. Gabel's recently published *The U.S. Army GHQ Maneuvers of 1941*, which had been given to him by Brigadier General Harold W. Nelson, the Chief of Military History.[41] In the early stage, Sullivan was simply searching for a label for a mode of experimentation. This mode of experimentation would help determine the direction the Army needed to move in.[42] In early November, General Sullivan and General Franks discussed the need to create some new mechanism to experiment with change. During that conversation, Franks referenced the Louisiana Maneuvers and the Howze Board studies on air assault concepts as two useful precedents.[43] Both were interested in the creation of a new training/experimentation platform, but they would part company over the proper location of this platform within the institutional Army. In December 1991, during a tour of the National Simulation Center at Fort Leavenworth, Sullivan directed Combined Arms Center Commander Lieutenant General Wilson Shoffner to conduct an analysis of the possibility of conducting an Army-wide maneuver in 1994 which would link together emerging simulation capabilities at Leavenworth, the Army War College, and the major commands.

Sullivan also knew that in a period of retrenchment, it would be critical to keep his senior commanders on board and prevent any in-house sniping that could undermine needed reforms. In order to facilitate agreement, Sullivan created a Board of Directors for the Louisiana Maneuvers made up of all the Army's four star generals who would "prioritize and sanction" the changes needed in the Army.[44] Acting under advice from Shoffner and TRADOCs analysis division, Sullivan created a Louisiana Maneuvers Task Force. In order to balance General Franks' desire that TRADOC serve as the primary architect for change with Sullivan's own desire to maintain direction of the project, the Louisiana Maneuvers Task Force was set up directly under the office of the Chief of Staff, with Franks serving as Deputy Director of the Maneuvers.[45] Further, the Task Force was co-located with TRADOC Headquarters at Fort Monroe. In May 1992, General Sullivan announced that Brigadier General Tommy Franks, then Assistant Commandant of the Field Artillery School, would become Executive Director of the Task Force.[46] Brigadier General Tommy Franks headed up the Task Force from 1992-94, and was succeeded by Brigadier General David H. Ohle.[47] The Louisiana Maneuvers Task Force eventually morphed into the Force XXI Task Force. The emphasis on using battle labs to explore the future of the Army's mission environment remained strong throughout the 1990s.[48]

The Debate Intensifies

In December 1992 the Bush administration, with tacit approval from President-elect Bill Clinton, committed 25,000 US troops to provide security for a UN humanitarian mission to Somalia.[49] During the following summer, the original humanitarian mission merged into a broader nation-building effort championed by UN Secretary General Boutros Boutros-Ghali. This effort involved an attempt to disarm Somalia's factitious warlords. The UN efforts prompted Mohammed Farah Aidid, the country's leading warlord, to battle UN forces, dragging the original humanitarian mission into the country's factional fighting.[50] Bereft of clear direction from Washington, US forces in Somalia soon became committed to trying to hunt down and capture Aidid. In an effort to capture Aidid and his senior lieutenants, US Army Rangers and elite Delta Force soldiers launched a raid into the heart of Aidid's territory in Mogadishu on 3 October 1993. Hovering over the urban terrain in support of the operation, two Black Hawk helicopters were shot down. What had begun as a quick snatch and grab raid quickly devolved into a more complicated extraction of the American forces. As Somali militia descended on the chaos, an intense urban firefight ensued in which 18 American soldiers were killed and 74 were wounded. Somali casualties ran into the hundreds.[51] For President Clinton, 3 October 1993 marked "one of the darkest days of my presidency." He wrote in his memoirs that "the Battle of Mogadishu haunted me."[52] Amidst widespread calls for the immediate withdrawal of US troops, the President and Congress settled on a compromise which called for the withdrawal of American forces on a strict six-month time limit.

Frustrations over US military intervention policy, highlighted by the tragedy in Somalia, prompted both Congress and the Clinton administration to undertake extended reviews of US military policy.[53] Congress mandated in the FY 1994 National Defense Authorization Act that the Department of Defense create a Commission on the Roles and Missions of the Armed

Services. The Commission was to prepare a report on these wide-ranging issues within a year of its formation. The Commission was placed under the direction of John P. White, a deputy of the newly appointed Secretary of Defense, William Perry.[54] The final report was finished by the spring of 1995.[55] The Clinton national security team undertook a narrower study on US intervention policy.[56] This resulted in the promulgation of Presidential Decision Directive 25 (PDD 25), "U.S. Policy on Reforming Multilateral Peace Operations."[57] It was issued on 3 May 1994, two months after General Sullivan had launched the Force XXI campaign.

The report of the Commission on Roles and Missions of the Armed Forces, titled *Directions for Defense*, was released just over a year later on 24 May 1995. The Pentagon took several additional months before adopting a formal position on the report. Secretary of Defense Perry transmitted his recommendations based on the report to Senator Strom Thurmond, Chairman of the Senate Committee on Armed Services, in late August. Perry strongly supported the Commission's recommendations for improving the effectiveness of unified operations. Perry advocated the "creation of an operational vision for joint operations" to be completed by the Chairman of the JCS by the fall [Joint Vision 2010]. In addition, the Joint Staff was henceforth responsible for the "development and implementation of joint doctrine." Perry also concurred with the need to provide greater support and resources to the unified commanders. Reflecting the tone of PDD 25, Perry wrote that the use of military forces in OOTW [Operations Other Than War] "should be limited to those tasks that are not more appropriately assigned to other elements of the government or private contractors." Specifically, Perry rejected any notion that US military forces should be engaged in the training of foreign constabulary forces.[58]

Force XXI Campaign

The Force XXI campaign was an attempt to transform the Army from a twentieth century industrial-age Army into a twenty-first information age Army. This was to be accomplished through redesigns of both the operational and institutional Army and introduction of digital technology into the active force.[59] The goal of Force XXI was the creation of Army XXI. The Force XXI campaign was officially launched by General Sullivan on 8 March 1994.[60] The Force XXI process proceeded along three axes. The operating force redesign was coordinated by TRADOC and known as JOINT VENTURE. It was to proceed with experiments at the brigade level, then division, then echelons above division. The redesign of the institutional Army was supervised by the Vice Chief of Staff of the Army.

The digitization of Army operational units was directed by the newly established Army Digitization Office. The Louisiana Maneuvers Task Force was then given "the mission of synchronizing and integrating the three Force XXI axes."[61] In the emerging multifaceted environment, the Force XXI campaign aimed to create an Army defined by: "doctrinal flexibility, strategic mobility, tailorability and modularity, joint and multinational connectivity, and the versatility to function in War and OOTW."[62]

In August 1994 TRADOC issued a pamphlet on Force XXI operations. TRADOC commander General William W. Hartzog later described it as "a think piece" and a "lighthouse of ideas" for future development.[63] The Force XXI Operations pamphlet stressed that "doctrine will remain the engine of change for Force XXI." TRADOC foresaw a need for doctrinal versatility in the coming years, calling for "*living* doctrine based on a fluid, strategic environment." Maintaining doctrinal relevance in such an environment was "the greatest intellectual challenge confronting the Army today."[64] A number of factors were to impact Force XXI Operations. One of the central features was the impact of information age technology, which was predicted to dramatically influence the tempo of operations. Access to information would also allow the force to be flattened—moving away from traditionally "stovepiped" or overly hierarchically organized formations. Indeed, Force XXI Operations foresaw knowledge-based land warfare achieving decisiveness in the early decades of the twenty-first century commensurate with blitzkriegs at the beginning of World War II.[65] In order to achieve this while developing a smaller force structure, the Army would have to place ever greater emphasis on a seamlessly integrated training system and leadership development. Officers were called upon to have a "broader understanding of war and the art of command," as well as "a higher level of doctrine-based skills, knowledge, attitudes, and experience to apply the battlefield operating systems to a wider range of complex contingency missions."[66] This suggests that TRADOC foresaw ever greater demands for Army officers' education.[67] Indeed, Force XXI Operations characterized the Army since 1989 as evolving into a "learning organization."[68] Organizationally the division was retained as "the major tactical formation," but with emphasis on tailorability and deployability for force projection operations.[69]

Doctrine as an Engine of Change?

One of TRADOCs responses to the need for versatile doctrine was the production of a new doctrinal manual on Peace Operations. Published in December 1994, FM 100-23, Peace Operations, amplified the chapter on

Operations Other than War in the 1993 edition of FM 100-5. It delineated three types of peace operations: 1) Support for diplomacy; 2) Peacekeeping; and 3) Peace enforcement. While FM 100-5 spoke of the continuum of operations, FM 100-23 emphasized that there was a clear distinction between peacekeeping and peace enforcement. Peacekeeping constituted neutral patrolling of a situation in which all concerned parties consented to the presence of the peacekeeping force. Conversely, peace enforcement called for the use of, or the threat of military force to impose sanctions or compel compliance with terms of a peace agreement. Typically peace enforcement activities were to take place under the umbrella of international authorization.[70] Despite the doctrinal innovation of FM 100-23, "training and preparation for peace operations should not detract from a unit's readiness to fight and win in combat."[71]

In October 1995 TRADOC Commander General William Hartzog initiated the fourth major rewrite of FM 100-5 since DePuy's 1976 edition. General Hartzog instructed the Combined Arms Center to undertake a new revision of FM 100-5 in the fall of 1995. General Hartzog's letter of instruction noted that one of the central points of working on a new edition was to spur the debate on "the very fundamentals of our profession." Hartzog saw this latest revision as an opportunity to advance the new "cycle" of doctrine that began with the 1993 edition, especially its development of the concepts of Operations Other Than War and Force Projection. Hartzog wanted to see both concepts more centrally integrated into the body of Army operational doctrine. OOTW in particular was to be integrated in such a way that the term itself could be dropped completely from the new manual.[72]

During the fall, Lieutenant General Leonard D. Holder, Jr., commander of the Combined Arms Center at Fort Leavenworth, began assembling a small, four man writing team.[73] The team was led by Lieutenant Colonel Michael Combest, who was a second year Advanced Operations Army Fellowship Program student when selected for the writing team. It also included Lieutenant Colonel Russell Glenn, a seminar instructor at SAMS, and Lieutenant Colonel Michael Burke, a SAMS exercise officer. Lieutenant General Holder also wanted Lieutenant Colonel David Fastabend, who was a fellow at the Hoover Institute in the fall of 1995. Fastabend did not join the team at Fort Leavenworth until late June 1996, though he had been in correspondence with Lieutenant Colonel Combest before his arrival. Fastabend sent his initial thoughts, whimsically titled "'Big Bites' or 'How to Start the Biggest Project of Our Otherwise Insignificant Lives'" to Lieutenant Colonel Combest on 12 May 1996. Given that the FM 100-5 writing team would be writing in an environment of plenty (of doctrine), which was also beginning to include joint doctrine as well as the profusion of TRADOC manuals, Fastabend was concerned about the problem of "doctrine glut." He defined this as "the generally unexpressed feeling that we have too many manuals that say too little." In order to break the deafening silence in the debate over doctrine induced by the "doctrine glut," Fastabend thought a number of considerations were in order. This included the need for a snappy name for the doctrine. He wrote that one of the 1982 editions' strengths had been its label "AirLand Battle," while the 1993 edition had suffered from a lack of a standout title. He also expressed a willingness to "shoot some sacred cows in the head" in order to stir up the doctrinal debate.[74]

By the middle of July 1996, the writing team presented some of its ideas on the new manual to Lieutenant General Holder. During this briefing, the new direction Lieutenant Colonel Fastabend had hinted at in his 12 May letter was made explicit. The team floated a concept for the new FM 100-5 as a "Land Dominance Operations" doctrine. The team defined Land Dominance, as "the ability to control, as required, terrain and the forces, populations, and situations on it."[75] It fulfilled the mandate laid out in FM 100-1; provided a comprehensive title for the full range of Army operations; reinforced the Army's unique responsibilities to the nation under Title 10 of the US Code; was in line with TRADOC 525-5 and Joint Vision 2010; and captured the essence off the current land forces debate.[76] In order to address General Hartzog's initial provision that OOTW not appear in the new doctrine and still address the full spectrum of operations called for in Joint Vision 2010, the team proposed a synthesis of the nine traditional principles of war with the six principles of Operations Other Than War which had been spelled out in the 1993 edition of FM 100-5. The new list was to be called the Principles of Operations. Two alternative lists of twelve principles each were proposed. The first six of the traditional principles of war (Objective, Maneuver, Economy of Force, Security, Simplicity, Surprise) remained unchanged. The next three (Offensive, Mass, and Unity of Command) were given alternatives. The team suggested Offensive be replaced with Initiative; Mass be replaced with Concentration or Massed Effects; and Unity of Command perhaps be changed to Unity of Effort. The remaining principles from OOTW in the 1993 edition were streamlined into Exploitation, Morale, and Sustainment/Legitimacy.[77] In the discussion over the briefing, Lieutenant General Holder made it clear that he did not want Land Dominance as the label for the new FM 100-5. He wanted greater stress on information operations and less on land dominance. Holder was also concerned about changing the principles of war. For the time being, he wanted the team to keep the Principles of War separate from the Principles of OOTW, while retaining the ability to fold them into a single list later.[78] Lieutenant General Holder did state his willingness to take up defense of the term "orchestration"—a phrase especially favored by Fastabend—to replace "synchronization" as a subject for change.[79]

In late July the commandants of each CAC school were briefed and encouraged to send comments by email as the draft got underway. In August the team busied themselves writing the first draft of the new FM 100-5. Among the materials the team drew on were the 1997 posture statements by the Secretary of the Army and Chief of Staff Dennis Reimer; USMC and British doctrinal manuals. FM 101-5-1 and TRADOC Force XXI documents also provided definitions of operations and patterns, respectively.[80] By early December the writing team had a chance to brief General Hartzog on its progress. The operational concept they presented to him was as follows:

> The Army's operational concept focuses on destroying enemy coherence. Serving as a primary land element of a joint and multinational force, Army units strike simultaneously throughout the battle space to control, neutralize, or destroy objectives whose loss disorganizes the enemy and breaks the coherence of his operations. Army units use information dominance, precision fires, superior relative mobility, and full force protection to conduct distributed, simultaneous, precise operations at a tempo and level of intensity enemy forces cannot match. These operations force the enemy into a turbulent, steadily deteriorating situation with which he cannot cope. His ability to conduct coordinated, effective operations is destroyed.
>
> Whether fighting a large, mechanized enemy, an elusive insurgency, or the effects of a natural disaster, our constant aim is to seize the initiative, maintain momentum, and exploit success in order to control the nature, scope and tempo of an operation. Army forces execute offensive, defensive, stability, and support operations through the aggressive, disciplined orchestration of the core functions See, Shape, Shield, Strike, and Move in ever changing combinations.[81]

In the ensuing discussion, General Hartzog stressed that he wanted more development of the scope of conflict in the operational concept, with special emphasis on preemptive employment and post-conflict operations. He generally supported the team's plan to fold the principles of war with the principles of OOTW into a single list. The core functions list, especially

Shield and Move, provoked additional comment. The ensuing discussion revolved primarily around the mechanics of when to present the draft to the broader Army audiences. It was decided for reasons of presentation to await the completion of the Advanced Warfighting Exercises then being conducted, and to begin briefing senior Army commanders. General Hartzog did make it clear, however, that General Reimer wanted to get the new FM 100-5 "done on his watch."[82] When General Reimer was formally briefed two months later, he supported the decision to begin distribution of an Army-wide coordinating draft in April 1997. He responded favorably to the single list of principles of operations, and after showing some hesitation about replacing synchronization with orchestration, stated his willingness to go along and see what the Army thought about the new term.[83]

In early April 1997 the distribution of the coordinating draft began Army-wide. Colonel Fastabend published an article in *Army* magazine advertising its pending arrival.[84] During the remainder of the spring and early summer, the writing team won generally positive response for the new manual. There was a definite sense that many people felt the effort of revising doctrine was well worth it. But within a few months the sense of confidence in a project nearing completion was to have the momentum completely taken out of it. The original writing team was dispersing for new assignments in the summer, replaced by a second team whose initial mission was only to shepherd the project through its final revisions and see it to press. Not only was the writing team changing hands, but CAC Commander Lieutenant General Holder retired from active duty on 1 September. His replacement, Lieutenant General Montgomery C. Meigs, saw fit to undertake a considerable revision of the FM 100-5 project. This decision meant that FM 100-5 was not released in late 1997 as had been originally planned. Under Lieutenant General Meigs' direction an entirely new draft of FM 100-5 was prepared over the following year, but it proved less acceptable to the Army at large.[85] It was not until late 1998 that yet another writing team began the revisions which resulted in the FM 3-0 which was finally released in 2001. As a result, the Army was not able to make use of the FM 100-5 revision as a successful driver of change as it had in the era of Active Defense and AirLand Battle.

From Quadrennial Review to Quadrennial Review

The Bush administration's Base Force levels were an attempt to establish a minimum level for US forces, but the levels it had established had quickly proven ephemeral. The Clinton administration's desire for greater cuts in defense spending and pressure in Congress to balance the federal budget both exerted considerable downward pressure on defense spending in the 1990s. The question after the 1993 Bottom-Up Review was thus how much farther reductions would go. The final report of the Commission on Roles and Missions of the Armed Forces for its part had little to say about adjusting force levels, per se. Congress provided the impetus for the next major analysis of force structure and strategy. The Military Force Structure Review Act of 1997, which was included in the annual National Defense Authorization Act for Fiscal Year 1997, instituted a Quadrennial Defense Review (QDR).[86]

The first such Quadrennial Defense Review was submitted under the imprimatur of Secretary of Defense William Cohen in May 1997. This was the second major defense review of the Clinton era, and the third major review since the Bush administration's Base Force review. It was designed to "be a fundamental and comprehensive examination of America's defense needs from 1997 to 2015."[87] The QDR presented three potential options to this question.[88] If the United States wanted to focus on security in the near term, particularly with an eye towards regional threats such as Iraq and Korea, then it made sense to stabilize force levels. The downside to the focus on the near term threats was that preparation for the long term (hence procurement) would suffer. Alternatively, the US could further trim down its active and reserve forces and reduce overseas commitments. This would provide money for a greater procurement program, and allow the United States to be better situated should a regional great power or a peer competitor emerge to challenge the US's superpower status ten to fifteen years in the future.[89] The downside, according to the QDR, would be an erosion of US influence and leadership in the near term, coupled with the danger of greater regional instability. Perhaps not surprisingly, the recommendation of the 1997 QDR struck a middle path between these two options. For the Army, the 1997 QDR advocated retention of a 10-division active force (6 heavy, 4 light, and 2 separate armored cavalry regiments), with a reduction of 15,000 active and 45,000 reserve personnel. At the same time, it called for an acceleration of the Force XXI modernization program. The Army was to retain the capability to "be able to deter and defeat large-scale, cross-border aggression in two distant theaters in overlapping time frames."[90] This focus on being able to deal with what were referred to as two major theater conflicts was characteristic of planning in the 1990s.

As the Army underwent reduction in size in the 1990s, it was clear that the perennial questions of the appropriate mix and form of divisions would have to be addressed. In order to facilitate the development of the new battlefield technologies, Army Chief of Staff General Sullivan designated the 2d Armored Division at Fort Hood, Texas as the Army's Experimental Force (EXFOR). In its capacity as the Army's experimental division, the 2d Armored was subsequently reflagged as the 4th Infantry Division. It served as a testbed for the new digitization technologies being considered for Army XXI.[91] The divisional breakdown of the late Cold War Army had favored heavy divisions, with considerable armor and mechanized forces. Initially the 10-division Army of 1996 was to be composed of 1 air assault, 1 airborne, 2 light, and 6 heavy divisions.[92] But the force projection Army of the 1990s placed a much higher premium on mobility, thus increasing the need for a better ratio of light or medium divisions in the overall Army force structure.[93] Writing in the fall of 1996, Army Chief of Staff General Reimer wrote that he expected the transformation to Army XXI to continue till 2010.[94] In 1999, Army Chief of Staff General Eric Shinseki would make speeding the pace of transformation to a more mobile, medium force central to his agenda. These new medium forces were to be based around an Interim Brigade Combat Team (IBCT). The IBCT were later renamed Stryker Brigade Combat Teams, or simply Stryker Brigades, after the new eight-wheeled infantry combat vehicles which they were equipped with. They were created by converting both existing light and heavy brigades, starting with two units at Fort Lewis, Washington.[95]

By the end of the first decade after the end of the Cold War, attention was increasingly focused on the issues of joint operations and military transformation.[96] The notion that the military might be undergoing a revolution in military affairs as industrial-age warfare gave war to information-age warfare has received considerable traction.[97] With personnel, deployment, and training costs consuming significant portions of the defense budget, modernizing the Army's equipment was also a major challenge.[98] The numerous studies undertaken in the 1990s had done little to provide definitive solutions to these problems, and indeed the bane of policy makers may well be the endless profusion of studies which offer options, without committing themselves to clear choices. With another Quadrennial Defense Review (QDR) scheduled for 2001, whichever new administration was elected in the 2000 elections would have an opportunity to find out if another round of review and study could prove in more successful.

Anticipating this issue, Chairman of the Joint Chiefs of Staff General Hugh Shelton initiated a review (or preview) of the upcoming QDR at the National Defense University in the fall of 1999 by a Quadrennial Defense Working Group directed by Michéle Flournoy.[99] As the study pointed out, both the Bottom-Up Review in 1993 and the QDR in 1997 had made planning for two-major theater wars "the highest priority mission assigned to the US military." The problem was that different types of major theater wars, with different types of desired end-states, could produce a wide-range of estimates for needed forces.[100] Defense against Iraqi and North Korean aggression and the re-establishment of existing international borders were the most often cited scenarios for potential major theater wars. But as the Working Group prophetically pointed out, should a major theater war involve removing an aggressive regime from power and then undertaking post-conflict stabilization, it "would require substantially more forces and time to execute" than mere restoration of borders and imposition of sanctions.[101] In order to come to a better understanding of what future force postures were appropriate, the Working Group called for a "rigorous and transparent methodology for assessing risk" as a central tenet of the next QDR.[102]

The 2001 QDR was approved by Secretary of Defense Donald Rumsfeld after several months of high level discussion and review within the Department of Defense.[103] The final report was released a few weeks after the September 11th terrorist attacks on New York and Washington. In his foreward to the report, Secretary of Defense Rumsfeld wrote:

> In important ways, these attacks confirm the strategic direction and planning principles that resulted from this review, particularly its emphasis on homeland defense, on surprise, on preparing for asymmetric threats, on the need to develop new concepts of deterrence, on the need for a capabilities-based strategy, and on the need to balance deliberately the different dimensions of risk.[104]

During hearings on the US National Security Strategy in the summer of 2001, Rumsfeld discussed the reasons he felt it was time to move beyond the two major theater war planning scenario which had been *en vogue* since the end of the Cold War.[105] Rumsfeld told the Senate Armed Services Committee that he felt the Two Major Theater War focused "planners on the near term to the detriment of preparing for longer-term threats." He likened post-Cold War planning to the "poverty of expectations; a routine obsession with a few dangers that may be familiar rather than likely," that Thomas Schelling had identified in reference to the US government's failures prior to the Pearl Harbor.[106] In order to better order US priorities for homeland defense and preparation for asymmetric threats while explicitly rejecting a neo-isolationist defense posture, the 2001 QDR called for a "paradigm shift" in the method of risk assessment.[107]

Instead of the threat-based risk assessments which had driven past planning, in Rumsfeld's Pentagon future force planning would derive from capabilities-based risk assessments. During the Cold War, when the Soviet Union was always seen as the primary adversary, threat-based analysis had been the order of the day. But in an environment where the United States could not know with confidence which state or combination of states or non-state actors would pose a threat in the long-term, it seemed to make more sense to plan instead for the type of capabilities that future adversaries would be able to employ.[108] The capabilities-based approach to force planning has remained one of the lasting initiatives of the 2001 QDR.[109] The QDR also called for "maintaining *regionally tailored forces* [emphasis in original] forward stationed and deployed in Europe, Northeast Asia, the East Asian littoral, and the Middle East/Southwest Asia to assure allies and friends, counter coercion, and deter aggression against the United States, its forces, allies, and friends."[110] Though not specifically expressed as such, the notion of regionally tailored forces was reminiscent of former Secretary of Defense Laird's "Strategy for Realistic Deterrence" of 1970. Given the ongoing demands on the military's force structure in the Global War on Terror, it is unclear to what extent the regional tailoring of the force structure has been able to proceed.[111]

Summary

During its first decade after the Cold War, the United States Army suffered from the same difficulties that national policy makers did in envisioning future environments. In contrast to earlier periods surveyed here, there was a distinct lack of executive consensus regarding the grand strategy to be pursued by the United States. In this context, the Army and the military writ large gave increasing attention to the issue of transforming themselves into a post-industrial, digital-age force. Like the promise of atomic age technology in the 1950s, the transformation efforts in the 1990s seldom met the promise of expectations. With lackluster executive guidance and military transformation mired in the promise of a technological revolution, the Congressional branch of government played an important role in guiding military adaptation during the 1990s.

Notes

1. Edward N. Luttwak, "A Post-Heroic Military Policy," *Foreign Affairs*, v.75, n.4 (July-August 1996), pp.35-36.

2. Clark, *Waging Modern War*, especially pp.416-44. For a perceptive analysis on how the shift in the perception of modern war from the older concept of total war had impacted academic military history, see Hew Strachan, "Essay and Reflection: On Total War and Modern War," *The International History Review*, v.XXII, n.2 (June 2000), pp.341-70.

3. Richard Lock-Pullan suggests that the Army had needed twenty years to address the "lessons" of Vietnam. Hence, it was hardly surprising that it was unable to adapt effectively in the changing environment of the 1990s. Lock-Pullan, *US Army Intervention Policy and Army Innovation*, p.195.

4. Linn, *The Echo of Battle*, pp.223-24.

5. A few caveats are in order. There may be a decided tendency to read unpreparedness (or perceived unpreparedness) for counterinsurgency in Iraq into the critique of the 1990s, which should remind us to be cautious of judging the past too exclusively by a present-centered concerns. In any case, this is an era in which the availability of archival evidence is very limited and one which the historiography is still rather limited. It is certainly worth noting that the debate itself transcends American politics, and is one which concerns all members of the world community. For a British perspective, see Rupert Smith, *The Utility of Force: The Art of War in the Modern World* (New York: Alfred A. Knopf, 2005).

6. Two useful analyses of different aspects of the strategy dilemma in this era include: David Jablonsky, "Army Transformation: A Tale of Two Doctrines," *Parameters*, v.XXXI, n.3 (Autumn 2001), pp.43-62; and Richard Meinhart, *Strategic Planning by the Chairmen, Joint Chiefs of Staff, 1990-2005* (Carlisle, PA: Strategic Studies Institute, April 2006).

7. McCormick, *The Downsized Warrior*, pp.36-37.

8. *Department of the Army Historical Summary: FY 1995*, p.38.

9. Though the Reagan Administration if often remembered for its massive defense build-up, defense spending was already declining in the latter years of the Reagan era. According to then Chief of Staff Carl Vuono, the FY 1992 budget represented the 7th straight year of real budgetary decline in spending on defense. Carl. E. Vuono, "National Strategy and the Army of the 1990s," *Parameters*, v.XXI, n.2 (Summer 1991), p.4.

10. This was best exemplified by Robert H. Scales, et. al., *Certain Victory: The US Army in the Gulf War* (Washington, DC: Office of Chief of Staff United States Army, 1993). Army Chief of Staff Carl Vuono wrote in the summer of 1991 that, "AirLand Battle doctrine proved its mettle in the deserts of Iraq and Kuwait." Carl E. Vuono, "National Strategy and the Army of the 1990s," *Parameters*, v.XXI, n.2 (Summer 1991), p.11.

11. Lock-Pullan, *US Army Intervention Policy and Army Innovation*, p.141.

12. For a good overview of military missions in the 1990s, see David Halberstam, *War in a Time of Peace: Bush, Clinton, and the Generals* (New York: Scribner, 2001).

13. Also see Thomas K. Adams, *The Army After Next: The First Postindustrial Army* (Westport, CT: Praeger, 2006).

14. For a succinct overview of the Act and its background, see Association of the United States Army, *Goldwater-Nichols Department of Defense Reorganization Act of 1986-A Primer* (Arlington, VA: Association of the United States Army, 1988), pp.2-5.

15. Ibid., p.13.

16. Ibid., p.16.

17. Ibid., p.35.

18. Robert M. Gates, "Beyond Guns and Steel: Reviving the Nonmilitary Instruments of American Power (Landon Lecture series)," *Military Review*, v.LXXXVIII, n.1 (January-February 2008), p.5.

19. McCormick, *The Downsized Warrior*, p.34. See also "A Talk with the Chief," *Army*, v.45, n.6 (June 1995), p.21.

20. Powell relates his original thinking for defense reductions, which included an Army of 525,000 men, began taking shape on 4 November 1989. Colin Powell, *My American Journey*, with Joseph E. Persico (New York: Random House, 1995), pp.435-36, 450-52.

21. Ibid., p.157.

22. McCormick, *The Downsized Warrior*, pp.36-37, and Powell, *My American Journey*, pp.457-58. For a more in-depth analysis, see Don M. Snider, *Strategy, Forces and Budgets: Dominant Influences in Executive Decision Making, Post-Cold War, 1989-91* (Carlisle, PA: Strategic Studies Institute, February 1993).

23. This emphasis on power projection also echoed Robert McNamara's program for the rapid redeployment of forces to US Army, Europe. It was first practiced in Operation BIG LIFT, and eventually grew into the REFORGER series of exercises.

24. Interestingly, Chief of Staff General Carl Vuono, in an article in *Parameters* dealing with the President's challenge for a new national strategy put a rather stronger spin on the need to quickly reconstitute/expand the force structure that was evident in President Bush's 2 August address. Vuono, "National Strategy and the Army of the 1990s," in, *Parameters*, p.5.

25. George Bush, Remarks at the Aspen Institute Symposium in Aspen, Colorado, 2 August 1990, p.3. John Woolley and Gerhard Peters, The American Presidency Project [online]. Santa Barbara, CA: University of California (hosted), Gerhard Peters (database). Available from World Wide Web: (http://www.presidency.ucsb.edu/ws/?pid=18731).

26. Vuono, "National Strategy and the Army of the 1990s," p.7.

27. Ibid., pp.10-11.

28. McCormick, *The Downsized Warrior*, p.39.

29. John L. Romjue, *American Army Doctrine for the Post-Cold War* (Fort Monroe, VA: Military History Office, TRADOC, 1997), pp.26-27, 31.

30. Ibid., p.33.

31. James L. Yarrison, *The Modern Louisiana Maneuvers* (Washington, DC: Center of Military History, 1999), pp.2-3.

32. Ibid., pp.35-36. For earlier Sullivan views on the role of doctrine, see Gordon Sullivan, "Doctrine: An Army Update," in, *The United States Army: Challenges and Missions for the 1990s*, pp.78-85.

33. General Sullivan responded to a question about vision statements in an interview with AUSA President General (ret.) Jack N. Merritt that, "My better judgment said that doctrine is the basis for all else, and the process of writing doctrine is important because leaders have to come together to write doctrine." See "A Talk with the Chief," *Army*, v.45, n.6 (June 1995), p.17.

34. Romjue, *American Army Doctrine for the Post-Cold War*, p.51.

35. James R. McDonough, "Building the New FM 100-5: Process and Product," *Military Review*, v.LXXI, n.10 (October 1991), pp.2-12; Gordon R. Sullivan, "Doctrine: A Guide to the Future," *Military Review*, v.LXXII, n2 (February 1992), pp.2-9; On doctrine for lower intensity conflicts, see the entire issue of *Military Review*, v.LXXII, n.4 (April 1992).

36. Romjue, *American Army Doctrine for the Post-Cold War*, pp.51-53.

37. Ibid., pp.60-61.

38. FM 100-5 (1993 edition), sec.1, pp.2-3.

39. Ibid., sec.1, p.4.

40. TRADOC Pamphlet 525-5, *Force XXI Operations: A Concept for the Evolution of Full-Dimensional Operations for the Strategic Army of the Early Twenty-First Century*, 1 August 1994, sec. 1, p.3.

41. Sullivan discussed the influence of Gabel's book and his motivations for initiating the Louisiana Maneuvers in an interview with AUSA President General (ret.) Jack N. Merritt. In addition to Gabel's book, Sullivan said he was influenced by Robert Doughty's *Seeds of Disaster* (Hamden CT: Archon Books, 1986) and *America's First Battles*, edited by Charles E. Heller and William A. Stofft (Lawrence, KS: University Press of Kansas, 1986). "A Talk with the Chief," *Army*, v.45, n.6 (June 1995), pp.17-18, 22. See also Yarrison, *The Modern Louisiana Maneuvers*, pp.12-13. There was a certain ambiguity in Gabel's conclusion about what the first Louisiana Maneuvers had taught the Army. Gabel wrote in his conclusion that "Although originally conceived as a training device, the GHQ maneuvers had their most lasting impact in the area of doctrine." A few pages later, he wrote: "in the final analysis, were the GHQ maneuvers worthwhile? The advances made in unit training proved ephemeral, relatively few maneuvers-trained commanders ever saw combat, and as a doctrinal laboratory the maneuvers ultimately proved

to be a mixed success." Christopher R. Gabel, *The U.S. Army GHQ Maneuvers of 1941* (Washington, DC: Center of Military History, 1991), pp.188, 192.

42. "A Talk with the Chief," *Army*, v.45, n.6 (June 1995), p.18.

43. Yarrison, *The Modern Louisiana Maneuvers*, pp.12-13.

44. "A Talk with the Chief," *Army*, v.45, n.6 (June 1995), pp.18-20.

45. Sullivan saw the LAM as directly part of his office. It was located "at" TRADOC, but not "in" it. See "A Talk with the Chief," *Army*, v.45, n.6 (June 1995), p.20.

46. Ibid., p.20.

47. Tommy Franks, *American Soldier*, with Malcolm McConnell (New York: Regan Books, 1994), pp.166-77.

48. Frederick M. Franks, Jr., *Battle Labs: Maintaining the Edge* (Fort Monroe, VA: Headquarters, US Army Training and Doctrine Command, May 1994).

49. For an account of US military operations, see Robert F. Baumann and Lawrence A. Yates, with Versalle F. Washington, *"My Clan Against the World": US and Coalition Forces in Somalia 1992-1994* (Fort Leavenworth, KS: Combat Studies Institute Press, 2004). On Bush-Clinton consultation, see Bill Clinton, *My Life* (New York: Alfred A. Knopf, 2004), p.550.

50. For a succinct account, see David Halberstam, *War in a Time of Peace: Bush, Clinton, and the Generals* (New York: Simon and Schuster, 2001), pp.248-61.

51. For the best account of the battle itself, see Mark Bowden, *Black Hawk Down: A Story of Modern War* (New York: Atlantic Monthly, 1999).

52. Clinton, *My Life*, p.552

53. The Bottom-Up Review, which had been conducted by Clinton's first Secretary of Defense, Les Aspin, had just been completed in September. The Bottom-Up Review had primarily focused on force structure, and less on roles and missions. For the Army, the Bottom-Up Review resulted in a reduction from 12 to 10 active divisions and set active end strength at 495,000 men. Les Aspin, *Report on the Bottom-Up Review*, October 1993, available at: http://www.fas.org/man/docs/bur/. See also, McCormick, *The Downsized Warrior*, pp.39-51.

54. Les Aspin announced his resignation on 15 December 1993. Peter Grier, "Aspin Departure Signals Shift in White House Defense Priorities," *The Christian Science Monitor*, 17 December 1993, p.2. Initially ADM (ret.) Bobby Ray Inman was nominated by Clinton to succeed Aspin, but when this appointment did not work out, Clinton turned to Aspin deputy William Perry. In his memoirs, former President Clinton glowingly wrote that, "[Perry] would turn out to be one of my best appointments, probably the finest secretary of defense since George C. Marshall." Clinton, *My Life*, p.576.

55. John P. White, et. al. *Directions for Defense: Report of the Commission on Roles and Missions of the Armed Forces* (Washington, DC: US Government Printing Office, 2005).

56. Other than his comment that he was "haunted" by the battle of Mogadishu, Clinton says little about the review of US intervention policy conducted by his NSC staff in his memoirs. See Clinton, *My Life*, pp.552ff.

57. Presidential Decision Directive 25, "US Policy on Reforming Multilateral Peace Operations," 6 May 1994. Available at: http://www.fas.org/irp/offdocs/pdd25.htm.

58. Ltr: Secretary of Defense William Perry to Strom Thurmond, 24 August 1995 with enclosure. DOD FOIA, ref. # 95-F-1939. Available at: http://www.dod.mil/pubs/foi/other/.

59. *Department of the Army Historical Summary: FY 1995*, p.37, and David H. Ohle, "The Campaign Plan," *Army*, v.45, n.2 (February 1995), pp.18-20. For a critical view of this attempt at transformation and Sullivan's vision for it, see Frederick W. Kagan, *Finding the Target: The Transformation of American Military Policy* (New York: Encounter Books, 2006), pp.166-75, and 201-05.

60. *Transforming the Army: TRADOC's First Thirty Years 1973-2003* (Fort Monroe, VA: Military History Offices, USA TRADOC, 2003), chap.3; and Hawkins and Carafano, *Prelude to Army XXI*, p.27.

61. *Department of the Army Historical Summary: FY 1995*, p.37.

62. TRADOC Pamphlet 525-5, Force XXI Operations, sec.3, p.1.

63. William W. Hartzog, "A 'Lighthouse of Ideas' on the Road to force XXI," *Army*, v.45, n.10 (October 1995), pp.55-59.

64. TRADOC Pamphlet 525-5, Force XXI Operations, sec. 4, pp.1-2.

65. Ibid., sec.3, p.19.

66. Ibid., sec.4, p.4.

67. Six years later Chairman of the Joint Chiefs of Staff, General Harry Shelton argued that "Regardless of budgetary and other constraints, our service and joint educational programs must remain top priorities." Harry H. Shelton, "Professional Education: The Key to Transformation," *Parameters*, v.XXXI, n.3 (Autumn 2001), p.15. For an appraisal of the Army War College curriculum in the 1990s, see Judith Hicks Stiehm, *The U.S. Army War College: Military Education in a Democracy* (Philadelphia: Temple University Press, 2002), pp.145-66.

68. TRADOC Pamphlet 525-5, Force XXI Operations, sec. 4, p.11.

69. Ibid., sec.4, p.5.

70. For a discussion of FM 100-23, see the article by TRADOC's Deputy Chief of Staff for Doctrine Morris J. Boyd, "Peace Operations: A Capstone Doctrine," *Military Review*, v.LXXV, n.3 (May-June 1995), pp.20-29.

71. Boyd, "Peace Operations: A Capstone Doctrine," p.28.

72. Ltr. from General William W. Hartzog to Lieutenant General Leonard D. Holder, Jr., 27 October 1995. CADD Office Files, Folder: 1998 FM 100-5, History, vol.I, tab.A. I am grateful to Colonel (ret.) Michael Burke, CADD, for making available his office files which contain a wealth of material on the 1995-2000 efforts to update FM 100-5.

73. General Hartzog had emphasized in his initial instructions that he wanted to avoid a manual with a "committee" approach and aim for a more homogeneous product.

74. Ltr. from Lieutenant Colonel David Fastabend to Lieutenant Colonel Michael Combest, "'Big Bites' or 'How to Start the Biggest Project of Our Otherwise Insignificant Lives,'" 12 May 1996. CADD Office Files, Folder: 1998 FM 100-5, History, vol.I, tab.H.

75. "Crossing the Line of Departure," FM 100-5 Writing Team Status Report Briefing for Lieutenant General Holder, 18 July 1996, slide 10. CADD Office Files, Folder: 1998 FM 100-5, History, vol.I, tab .O.

76. Ibid., slide 11.

77. Ibid., slide 12.

78. "Summary of Remarks, 18 July 1996 FM 100-5 Briefing to Lieutenant General Holder," CADD Office Files, Folder: 1998 FM 100-5, History, vol.I, tab. O.

79. Ibid.

80. Memo, Continuity Aid from Russell Glenn, 1998 FM 100-5 Author [undated]. CADD Office Files, Folder: 1998 FM 100-5, History, final volume [unlabeled]. In this 3 page memo, Lieutenant Colonel Glenn spelled out which sections of the manual he served as primary author on, and discussed those materials which influenced him.

81. Upon seeing the slide, General Hatzog exclaimed, "Holy cow!" Briefing on FM 100-5 for General Hartzog, 10 December 1996. CADD Office Files, Folder 1998 FM 100-5, History, vol.IV, tab.G."

82. Ibid.

83. The eleven principles of operations were consistent in both briefs, and included: Objective, Offensive, Maneuver, Massed Effects, Economy of Force, Unity of Effort, Security, Morale, Simplicity, Surprise, and Exploitation. The operational concept had undergone editorial revision, which primarily resulted in the rearrangement of its structure. However, the introductory sentence changed to, "Army forces accomplish assigned missions worldwide by executing offensive, defensive, stability, and support operations." The five core functions (See, Shape, Shield, Strike, and Move), which were previously listed were removed. Briefing on FM 100-5 for General Reimer, 14 February 1997. CADD Office Files, Folder 1998 FM 100-5, History, [unlabelled], tab.XYZ."

84. David A. Fastabend, "FM 100-5, 1998: Endless Evolution," *Army*, v.47, n.5 (May 1997), pp.44-50.

85. Interview with Colonel (ret.) Michael Burke.

86. William S. Cohen, *Report of the Quadrennial Defense Review*, May 1997. Available at: http://www.dod.mil/pubs/qdr/index.html.

87. *Report of the Quadrennial Defense Review*, sec.1, p.1.

88. *Report of the Quadrennial Defense Review*, sec.4: Alternative Defense Postures.

89. Specifically, this path called for minimum reductions to defense manpower of 100,000 active, 110,000 reserve, and 90,000 civilian personnel. These reductions were to be compensated in the future by "revolutionary enhancement of US military technology." *Report of the Quadrennial Defense Review*, sec.4, p.4. For a more on the "revolutionary enhancements" in technology, see Defense Science Board 1996 Summer Study Task Force on *Tactics and Technology for 21st Century Military Superiority* (Washington, DC: Office of the Secretary of Defense, October 1996). DOD FOIA (Defense Science Board), available at: http://www.dod.mil/pubs/foi/dsb/.

90. *Report of the Quadrennial Defense Review*, sec.III, p.8.

91. For a discussion of the first Brigade Combat Team experiments of the 4th ID[M] at Fort Hood, Texas and the NTC, see Dennis Steele interview of Colonel Thomas R. Goedkoop, "Forging Task Force XXI," *Army*, v.46, n.11 (November 1996), pp.23-25, Thomas R. Goedkoop and Barry E. Venable, "Task Force XXI: An Overview," *Military Review*, v.LXXVII, n.2 (March-April 1997), and William W. Hartzog and Susan Canedy, "A Time for Transformation: Creating Army XXI," *Army*, v.46, n.10 (October 1996), pp.53-59.

92. Hawkins and Carafano, *Prelude to Army XXI*, p.27.

93. See John Gordon IV and Peter A. Wislon, *The Case for Army XXI "Medium Weight" Aero-Motorized Divisions: A Pathway to the Army of 2020* (Carlisle Barracks, PA: Strategic Studies Institute, May 1998); and John Gordon IV and Peter A. Wilson, "The Case for Medium-Weight Army Forces," *Army*, v.49, n.12 (December 1999), pp.33-40.

94. Dennis J. Reimer, "The U.S. Army: The World's Premier Force," *Army*, v.46, n.10 (October 1996), p.22.

95. William M. Donnelly, *Transforming an Army at War: Designing the Modular Force, 1991-2005* (Washington, DC: Center of Military History, Department of the Army, 2007), pp.10-11, and McGrath, *The Brigade*, p.107.

96. There is a good deal of valuable information on Army Transformation online, available at: http://www.comw.org/rma/fulltext/ustrans.html. For two useful collections, one published prior to the September 11th attacks, the other well into the Global War on Terror, respectively, see Williamson Murray, ed. *Army Transformation: a View from the U.S. Army War College* (Carlisle, PA: Strategic Studies Institute, July 2001), and John J. McGrath, gen. ed., *An Army at War: Change in the Midst of Conflict*. The Proceedings of the Combat Studies Institute 2005 Military History Symposium (Fort Leavenworth, KS: Combat Studies Institute Press, August 2005).

97. For an early critical analysis, see Steven Metz and James Kievit, *Strategy and the Revolution in Military Affairs: From Theory to Policy* (Carlisle, PA:

Strategic Studies Institute, 1995). There is a good deal of valuable information on the Revolution in Military Affairs online, available at: http://www.comw.org/rma/fulltext/reflect.html. The 2001 Quadrennial Defense Review stated, somewhat equivocally, that, "the ongoing revolution in military affairs could change the conduct of military operations. Technologies for sensors, information processing, precision guidance, and many other areas are rapidly advancing. This poses the danger that states hostile to the United States could significantly enhance their capabilities by integrating widely available off-the-shelf technologies into their weapons systems and armed forces. For the United States, the revolution in military affairs holds the potential to confer enormous advantages and to extend the period of US military superiority." Donald Rumsfeld, *Quadrennial Defense Review Report*, 30 September 2001 (Washington, DC: Department of Defense, 2001), p.6.

98. CSA Reimer wrote that, "we have really found ourselves in the past in a death spiral. In order to keep the Army trained and ready, we mortgaged the modernization account. Now we find ourselves in the position of having to trade off force structure in order to beef up the modernization account." Dennis J. Reimer, "'Soldiers Are Our Credentials': Today's Army," *Army*, v.46, n.2 (February 1996), p.18.

99. Michéle A. Flournoy (Project Director), *Report of the National Defense University Quadrennial Defense Review 2001 Working Group* (Washington, DC: Institute for National Strategic Studies, National Defense University, November 2000).

100. Also see Steven Metz, *American Strategy: Issues and Alternatives for the Quadrennial Defense Review* (Carlisle, PA: Strategic Studies Institute, September 2000), and Steven Metz, ed., *Revising the Two MTW Force Shaping Paradigm* (Carlisle, PA: Strategic Studies Institute, April 2001).

101. Flournoy, *Report of the National Defense University Quadrennial Defense Review 2001 Working Group*, p.11.

102. Ibid., p.47.

103. In the fall of 2000, President George W. Bush was narrowly elected president in a contentious election. He chose Donald Rumsfeld to serve as his Secretary of Defense. Rumsfeld had previously served as Secretary of Defense under President Gerald Ford from 1975 to 1977. On his tenure as Secretary of Defense in the Bush administration, see "Donald H. Rumsfeld, January 20, 2001-December 18, 2006, 21st Secretary of Defense," available at: http://www.defenselink.mil/specials/secdef_histories/; Mann, *Rise of the Vulcans*, pp.269-358; and Scarborough, *Rumsfeld's War*, passim.

104. Rumsfeld, *Quadrennial Defense Review Report* (2001), p.v.

105. Senate Armed Services Committee, *Hearing on U.S. National Security Strategy*, 21 June 2001, pp.4-5. Chaired by Senator Carl Levin (D-MI). Retrieved from LexisNexis Congressional Search. Rumsfeld made similar remarks to the

House Armed Services Committee later that day. Available at: http://commdocs. house.gov/committees/security/has172000.000/has172000_0.HTM.

106. Senate Armed Services Committee, *Hearing on U.S. National Security Strategy*, 21 June 2001, p.5.

107. See "The Paradigm Shift in Force Planning" in Rumsfeld, *Quadrennial Defense Review Report* (2001), p.17.

108. Rumsfeld, *Quadrennial Defense Review Report* (2001), pp.13-14.

109. The use of capabilities-based planning was reaffirmed in the 2005 National Defense Strategy and the 2006 QDR. Michael Fitzsimmons, "Whither Capabilities-based Planning?," *Joint Force Quarterly*, issue 44, (1st Quarter, 2007), pp.101-105.

110. Rumsfeld, *Quadrennial Defense Review Report* (2001), p.20.

111. For recent literature on the ongoing transformation initiatives, see Donnelly, *Transforming an Army at Wa*r, passim, Frederick W. Kagan, *Finding the Target: The Transformation of American Military Policy* (New York: Encounter Books, 2006), and Douglas A. Macgregor, *Transformation Under Fire: Revolutionizing How America Fights* (Westport, CT: Praeger, 2003).

Conclusion

In his classic study of the United States Army, Russell Weigley characterized the US Army on the eve of the Korean War as one wrapped in the traditions of its recent past. It was an Army "shaped less by military doctrine looking to a future war, to which this Army often seemed so irrelevant, than by the past, by the last war, of whose massive armies it was the remnant."[1] But the Army since the Korean War has called a rather different tune. More often than not the Army's attention after periods of extended conflict did in fact turn towards the future, and away from the experience of its recent past. In his study of Army lesson learning, Dennis Vetock charged that, "No lesson-learning system, beginning with American involvement in World War I, has survived beyond the particular war that gave it life."[2] After the Korean War the Army focused its attention on its role in the defense of NATO Europe, preparing to fight against a potential Soviet onslaught by employing the latest tools of technology, including tactical nuclear weapons. After Vietnam, the Army again refocused its attention on the European battlefield. More recently, Frederick Kagan has pointed out that "Army leaders saw Desert Storm as likely to be the last major ground conflict of its kind, and rejected the idea of building future force structures to fight similar wars in the future."[3] As General Donn Starry commented in 1978, "after every war, armies always set out to figure out how they might have fought the last war better. There was an even stronger determination to avoid that pitfall, and this time to look ahead, not back [towards Vietnam]."[4] Starry's comment exemplifies the trend in the post-World War II Army to conceive of itself as a future-looking organization. But this has often masked a tendency to turn away from the lessons of recent experience. There is no vantage on the future that does not ground itself in some past experience.[5] The Army's desire to turn away from its Korean War and Vietnam War experiences is symptomatic of this tendency to selectively use the past to look ahead. If past experience is used too exclusively, the Army runs the danger of forgetting that full-spectrum capabilities call for a full appreciation of its own variegated history. If there has been a poverty of expectations, it is because the Army forgets the full-range of its past experience.

Though the experience of the Korean War was not one which the US Army could or should have remembered fondly, the institution emerged from the conflict flush from the wartime buildup. Bloodied, but not beaten, the US Army had rebounded from the post-World War II reductions to a much improved position by 1952-53. Projected force levels for the defense of Western Europe provided the need for a long-term commitment to that continent. President Eisenhower's New Look national security policy, however, quickly dashed the hopes in the Army that the peacetime force would continue at the force levels achieved during the build-up from 1950-52. Instead, reliance on the deterrent power of the Strategic Air Command and a need to reduce inflated wartime budgets soon placed the Army in the uncomfortable position of once again having to adapt itself to reduced manpower and budgets. This downturn in resources, coupled with the President's views on future war, provoked sustained criticism from many within his old service. Most notably, President Eisenhower faced ongoing dissent from two successive Chiefs of Staff, Generals Matthew Ridgway and Maxwell Taylor. As a result, the Pentomic era is generally remembered for the discord in civil-military relations, failed experimentation with divisional reorganization, and over-preoccupation with a type of war which never occurred. While this perception is not completely incorrect, it does overlook a number of aspects of Army adaptation in this period which are worth revisiting.

While the need for immediate response in the New Look was fundamentally about assuring that Strategic Air Command got its bombers off early enough to destroy the Soviet bomber fleet on the ground, it did have an analog in Army readiness. The disaster of Task Force *Smith* (which was again trumpeted as an important lesson of the past in the 1990s) in the initial phase of the Korean War, coupled with the need to meet any Soviet assault on NATO Europe as far to the east as possible, gave the Army a viable reason to call for an immediate readiness. Its urgency was reinforced in the 1950s because the conception of future war with the Soviets would be characterized by an initial short, intense phase. The course of the war might well be decided in its opening month, week, or even days. There would therefore be little opportunity for the traditional breathing space in which the US suffered an initial reverse (e.g. Pearl Harbor, the Kasserine Pass, Task Force *Smith*), only to use the advantages of time and space to build-up and deploy a decisive force.

The primary challenge of the Pentomic age was the conceptual difficulty of dealing with a type of warfare for which there was no historical precedent, excepting only the destruction of Hiroshima and Nagasaki at the end of World War II. Many observers have noted that the Pentomic division seemed profoundly ill-suited for fighting the sort of sustained, heavy combat that had characterized fighting in Northwest Europe in World War II. But given Eisenhower's firm conviction—which he retained

112

throughout his presidency—that there would not be a limited war with the Soviets, and his conviction that the US should avoid future Korean-scale engagements, there was little danger that the Pentomic division would be employed in such a way to expose its weaknesses. Over time, its communications and transportation deficiencies might well have been rectified. Had this come to pass, the Pentomic structure might have proved to be a suitable enough structure for deployments on the types of operations short of war that Eisenhower considered appropriate uses of military force.

The debate about the Pentomic division in the late 1950s was the extent to which it was in fact dual-capable. The problem of dual-capability addressed a broader question. This problem was whether an entire army can be or should be geared for a single form of war. The essential question was whether or not organizing, training, and especially equipping for the nuclear battlefield made a division less-capable of fighting conventionally. The US Army's answer seems to lie in the rapidity with which the Pentomic division was abandoned when the presidential administration changed hands. The election of John F. Kennedy as president provided the opportunity for the Army to abandon the Pentomic division and distance itself from preoccupation with the tactical nuclear battlefield (though the issue of tactical nuclear weapons and the European battlefield would recur again in the decades to come). The Pentomic division was subsequently replaced by the ROAD division. With its ability to interchange battalions (both numbers and types) amongst its brigade headquarters, the ROAD division did indeed have a theoretical versatility which meshed well with the general approach of flexible response. It was theoretical because if units were not regularly rotated, force of habit could make ROAD's structure as inflexible as its predecessors. The new divisional structure, however, did not answer the question of whether or not ROAD was any more dual-capable than the Pentomic division. On balance, it would seem that the ROAD division was better suited for the sort of conventional warfighting at the upper-end of the conventional spectrum, but its dual-capability remained as academic as that of the Pentomic division.

The era of adaptation after the Vietnam War presented the Army with different challenges than those it had faced in the 1950s. The Army as an institution had to adapt to troop reductions, but this was hardly the greatest of its worries. The end of the draft meant the end to the Army's self-conception as the nation-in-arms made up of citizen-soldiers. This problem was compounded by the erosion of discipline and rampant drug use which characterized the Army in the waning years of the Vietnam conflict. The Army's response in the 1970s owed much to the leadership of generals like

Creighton Abrams, William DePuy, and Donn Starry. Abrams steadied the helm through the roughest years of the transition before his untimely death. DePuy and Starry provided focus for the Army's rebuilding by championing the conception of a doctrinally based Army and emphasizing realistic training. The embrace of doctrine and training as engines of change provided a useful focus for the Army as it rebuilt itself as an institution. Many of the changes adopted in this era remain part of the Army today. This is especially apparent in the Training and Doctrine Command. National training centers, battle labs, a considerable doctrine writing establishment, and institutionalized lesson learning have all been retained from this era's adaptations.

In the 1990s, the Army emerged from the first Gulf War and the end of the Cold War as an institution whose previous reforms in training and doctrine seemed vindicated by success. Nonetheless, success and the perceived dramatic changes in the international environment bred reductions in a way reminiscent of the demobilizations at the end of World War II, albeit on a smaller scale. Much like the period of the late-1940s, the international situation in the 1990s was difficult to predict. Indeed, the ongoing process of defense reviews which characterized much of the 1990s reflected not only domestic pressure to reap the peace dividend, but the difficulties faced by political and military leaders in addressing the age old question of the utility of military force. The Louisiana Maneuvers process initiated by General Gordon Sullivan was symptomatic of the perceived need to change, overlayed with the lack of clear direction about what that change should bring. Indeed, the long delays in publishing FM 100-5 in the later 1990s reflected the uncertainties the Army faced in this period.[6] Difficult missions abroad which lacked clear charters reinforced the sense that the nation needed to answer the question of utility of force and provided clearer direction to the military. Given the lack of clear direction from the executive branch in this regard, Congress' role in pressing for clearer guidelines for the national application of military power was especially pronounced in the 1990s. This trend certainly had its roots in the 1970s, when the collapse of the Nixon presidency and disquiet over Vietnam had resulted in increased Congressional involvement in foreign and defense policy. The Goldwater-Nichols Act of 1986 in some ways was the culmination of the first phase of this renewed Congressional involvement. In the 1990s, it was the intervention in Somalia which again prompted considerable Congressional involvement. The Commission on Roles and Missions of the Armed Forces and the creation of the Quadrennial Review process were both significant Congressional initiatives in this regard. Within the Army, adaptation/transformation which relied on institutionalized "engines of change" was not always successful. The problem of publishing a new edition of FM 100-5 in the later part of the decade is highly suggestive that the doctrinal revolution instituted by DePuy and Starry in the 1970s had lost its ability to mobilize change within the Army.

One of the central features that emerges is that any number of contemporary debates have historical antecedents. The long-standing debate over the primacy of offense or defense, which was renewed in 1953, prefigured the debates over Active Defense and AirLand Battle in the late 1970s and early 1980s. The 1950s debate over whether the Army could produce a viable dual-capable force (tactical nuclear war and conventional war), continued in the 1970s and has widened today into a discussion of how best to prepare the Army for a full-spectrum of contingencies. One of the "lessons" which emerged from the initial reverses of the Korean War, was that the Army needed to be "capable of immediate commitment." This too continues to resonate in the Army, which has placed a good deal of stress on training and readiness ever since.

When we compare the three eras surveyed here, it is important to note some distinguishing features. During the Eisenhower presidency and in the aftermath of the unpopular stalemate in Korea, both the President and the country had little taste for the use of force in limited war situations. The alleged revolution in military thought brought about by the nuclear era in which ground combat seemed to have much less relevance than in the recent past, made it difficult for the Army to make important doctrinal and force structure decisions about its future. Given that at its "nadir" in early 1961, there were still more than 850,000 men in the active Army, one could be forgiven for thinking the Army's senior leadership over-reacted in its strained relations with the executive. Most of the division experiments ended as dead ends. The curriculum at Leavenworth swung heavily in favor of the nuclear battlefield, but this emphasis proved to be a rather short-lived trend. Very few of the Army's changes in the Pentomic era lasted beyond the early 1960s. The Army's internal turmoil of the 1950s might best be seen as a cautionary tale of the dangers of getting too wrapped up about transforming for the future at the expense of remembering past experience.

In the 1970s the situation faced by the Army was more difficult. Though the Korean stalemate was less than ideal, it did not wreak the havoc on the institution that the Vietnam War did. Given the challenges faced by the Army in this decade, compared to either the 1950s or 1990s, the wide-ranging institutional response in the 1970s was rather impressive.

Much of the general institutional structure of the STEADFAST reorganization, the creation of an all volunteer force, and the doctrinal and training substructures which developed afterwards, remain part of the Army today. The perception of a clear and present threat from the Soviet Union and the Warsaw Pact served as the threat for which the Army prepared and trained. The rebuilding of the Army's effectiveness in the 1970s and 1980s, driven by fundamental institutional changes, was an impressive achievement.

The later 1990s, by contrast, seem more reminiscent of the 1950s, when strained civil-military relations and the chimera of a revolution in military affairs were the order of the day. It also important to remember that the decade began with the combined triumphalism of the collapse of America's Cold War rival and victory in the first Gulf War. Given the lack of a clearly defined military mission and a series of peacekeeping and unconventional operations, it is perhaps not surprising that both the country and the Army took some time to sort out future expectations. The concept of an amorphous, capabilities-based force replaced the old threat-based model that had driven Army doctrine, training, equipment and force structure just a decade earlier. Our understanding of civil-military relations and the extent to which the 1990s did or did not experience a revolution in military affairs will probably benefit from improved perspective with the passage of time.

If past experience is any guide, it is likely that the United States will again undergo a period of reflection and adaptation once the majority of troops are redeployed from current commitments in Afghanistan and Iraq. In the more distant future it is likely that Operations Other Than War (or whatever term they will then be known by) will be common contingencies for the US military. Barring a change to the current arc of US involvement in Iraq, the US Army institutionally is not likely to face the same degree of "inward looking" soul-searching that followed the Vietnam War. Recent calls for a return to "full-spectrum" capabilities remind one of the conclusions of the Astarita Report and DePuy's decision to orient the 1976 FM 100-5 almost wholly toward full-scale conventional operations on the European battlefield. If the Army is to gain insight from its previous periods of adaptation in the wake of prolonged campaigns (Korea, Vietnam, and the Cold War confrontation writ large), it might be that no matter how great the temptation to refocus Army-wide attention on a single potential type of warfare, that temptation should be resisted. It would be best to remember what really constitutes "full-spectrum" operations, and not to use this as a mere buzz word to mask prioritizing the types of short, intense, upper-end of the conflict spectrum, wars that the Army has demonstrated

116

a long standing institutional preference to focus on. For the next generation, the Army will benefit from a richly experienced officer corps that has indeed waged full-spectrum warfare from the first Gulf War to the alleys of Mogadishu to the streets of Baghdad. If it can remember, reflect, and learn from the entire variety of this experience, valuable learning will have indeed taken place.

Notes

1. Weigley, *History of the United States Army*, enlarged edition, p.502.
2. Vetock, *Lessons Learned: A History of US Army Lesson Learning*, p.120.
3. Kagan, *Finding the Target*, p.160.
4. Donn A. Starry, "A Tactical Evolution-FM 100-5," *Military Review*, v.LVIII, n.8 (August 1978), p.3.
5. For instance, when General DePuy turned his attention to the 1973 Arab-Israeli War as a vantage on the future, he succumbed to the very fault that Starry claimed was being avoided. In the mid-1970s, the most recent war was the Yom Kippur War, not Vietnam.
6. It might also indicate the extent to which the doctrinal revolution of the 1970s has played itself out as a driving force for change within the Army.

Appendix
Boards, Committees, Reviews, and Studies

European Theater of Operations, General Board (1945-46)
Gerow Board (1945)
Haislip Board (1945)
National Security Act (1947)
Eddy Board (1949)
Army Organization Act (1950)
Project SOLARIUM (1953) [President Eisenhower]
PENTANA Study (1955)
Williams Board (1958)
Hoelscher Committee (1961)
Traub Committee (1961)
Stillwell Report (1961)
ROAD (1961-62)
Howze Board (1962)
Haines Board (1965)
Parker Panel (1969-70)
CONARC Leadership Board (1971)
CONARC Board for Dynamic Training (1971)
Ad Hoc Committee on the Army Need
   for the Study of History (1971)
STEADFAST Reorganization (1973)
Total Force Study (1973)
Astarita Report (1974) [CSA General Westmoreland]
Division Restructuring Study (1975-1979)
Hollingsworth Report (1976)
A Study of Strategic Lessons Learned in Vietnam (1980)
RETO (1977-78)
Army 86 (1978-1983)
High Technology Light Division (HTLD) (1980-1984)
Project 14 (1983) [CSA General Wickman]
Army Staff College Level Training Study
   (1983) [Colonel Huba Wass de Czege]
Kupperman Study (1983)
Goldwater-Nichols Act (1986) [Congress]
Dougherty Board (1987)
Anteus Study (1989) [CSA General Carl Vuono]
Quicksilver I (1989)
Quicksilver II (1990)

Base Force Review (1991) [Bush administration]
New Louisiana Maneuvers (1992-94) [CSA General Gordon Sullivan]
Bottom-Up Review (1993) [SecDef Les Aspin]
Force XXI (1994-)
Commission on Roles and Missions of the Armed Forces (1995) [Congressionally mandated]
Army After Next (1996-)
Defense Science Board, 1996 Summer Study Task Force (1996)
Quadrennial Defense Review (1997) [Congressionally mandated, SecDef Cohen]
National Defense Panel (1997)
Quadrennial Defense Review (2001) [Congressionally mandated, SecDef Rumsfeld]

Ad Hoc Committee on the Army Need for the Study of History: Committee appointed by CSA General Westmoreland at the behest of retiring Chief of Military History Brigadier General Hal C. Pattison to inquire into the state of military history instruction in the US Army. The committee was chaired by Colonel Thomas E. Griess, Professor and Head of the Department of History at West Point.[1] (1971)

Anteus Study: Study initiated by CSA General Carl Vuono to review the Army's force structure, with emphasis on Europe, in the climate of a likely conventional force reduction treaty with the Soviets. The study, completed in October 1989, projected a decade long force reduction from 771,000 soldiers in 18 divisions to 640,000 soldiers in 15 divisions.[2]

Army After Next (1996-): Begun in February 1996 to look at the Army 30 years in the future.[3]

Army Organization Act of 1950:[4]

Army Science Board:[5] Commissioned on 15 May 1980 to study the development of a "high technology" division.[6]

Army Staff College Level Training Study: Report by Colonel Huba Wass de Czege that recommended the establishment of a second year of instruction at the Command and General Staff College focused on the operational art of war. This report, completed in June 1983, contributed to the establishment of the School of Advanced Military Studies at the CGSC.[7]

ASTARITA Report: General Creighton Abrams created a special Strategic Assessment Group in the spring of 1973 to determine what role there was for conventional forces in the post-Vietnam War. The Strategic

Assessment Group was headed by Abrams' confidant Colonel Edward F. Astarita.[8]

Base Force Review: A plan for force reductions iniated by Chairman of the Joint Chiefs, General Colin Powell. Powell earned President Bush's approval for the concept on 1 August 1991. The Base Force became the administration's official position for minimum future defense levels. It called for reductions in active duty end strength from 2.1 million to 1.6 million, with an active duty Army of 535,000 men and twelve divisions.[9]

Bottom-Up Review: Review initiated by Secretary of Defense Aspin shortly after coming to office. The final report was ready by 1 September 1993. It called for a reduction in defense posture consonant with President Clinton's campaign promise, though the initial cuts were smaller than some expected. The Army faced the largest cuts. The active force was trimmed from 12 divisions to 10.[10]

Combat Arms Training Board: Successor to CONARC's Board for Dynamic Training.

Commission on Roles and Missions of the Armed Forces: This Commission was mandated by Congress in the National Defense Authorization Act for FY 1994. It was headed by Secretary of Defense William Perry's deputy, John P. White. The Commission report was completed in late May 1995.[11] Secretary of Defense Perry then transmitted his recommendations to Congress based on the findings of the panel.[12]

CONARC Board for Dynamic Training: Established by General Westmoreland in September 1971. Its aim was to identify deficiencies in training techniques, devices and management. Its successor was the Combat Arms Training Board.[13]

CONARC Leadership Board: Established at Fort Bragg, NC in May 1971.[14]

Davies Committee:[15]

Defense Science Board: 1996 Summer Study Task Force on Tactics and Technology for 21st Century Military Superiority.[16]

Dougherty Board: "The Report of the Senior Military Schools Review Board on Recommendations to the Chairman of the Joint Chiefs of Staff Regarding Professional Military Education in Joint Matters," 7 May 1987.[17]

Eddy Board: General review of officer education conducted in 1949, headed by Leavenworth Commandant Lieutenant General Manton S.

Eddy. Report sent to Department of the Army in mid-June 1949.[18]

Gerow Board: War Department Military Education Board, chaired by Commandant of the Command and General Staff School, Lieutenant General Leonard T. Gerow. Approved by Chief of Staff Dwight D. Eisenhower on 23 November 1945, and given five weeks to report back on a plan for postwar Army education.[19]

Haines Board: Department of the Army review of officer education under the direction of Lieutenant General Ralph E. Haines, Jr. The review convened in July 1965 and completed its work six months later.[20] This board's work was bookended by the Army War College-70 study and the Assistant Secretary for Defense's (Manpower) Officer Education study.

Haislip Board (Board of Officers to Review War Department Policies and Programs): Under the direction of General Wade H. Haislip. Final report delivered on 25 April 1947.[21]

Hoelscher Committee (Project 80): Study of the Functions, Organization, and Procedures of the Department of the Army. It was placed under the direction of Deputy Comptroller of the Army Leonard W. Hoelscher. Its results were transmitted to the Chief of Staff on 5 October and to Secretary McNamara on 16 October 1961. Recommended creating a Systems and Material Command, a Combat Developments Command, and changing CONARC into a Force Developments Command. Its recommendations were modified by the Traub Committee Report.[22]

Hollingsworth Report: "An Assessment of Conventional War Fighting Capability and Potential of the US Army in Central Europe," 30 June 1976.[23]

Howze Board: US Army Tactical Mobility Requirements Board, chaired by Lieutenant General Hamilton H. Howze, commander of the XVIII Airborne Corps. The report, submitted on 20 August 1962, recommended the creation of an airmobile division.[24]

Kupperman Study: A TRADOC commissioned study by Robert Kupperman and Associates completed in 1983. It looked at military requirements for the world environment of the coming two decades.[25]

Louisiana Maneuvers: The attempt by CSA General Gordon Sullivan to harness emerging simulation technologies with traditional maneuvers and experimentation into a new process of adaptation for the US Army. CSA Sullivan's choice of the Louisiana Maneuvers harkened back to the pre-World War II maneuvers held in Louisiana in 1941. A task force under this name operated to coordinate the simulations, battlelabs, and wargam-

122

ing experiments between 1992 and 1994. Much of what made up the Louisiana Maneuvers eventually morphed into the Force XXI Campaign.[26]

National Defense Panel: Produced a Congressionally-mandated report on the 1997 Quadrennial Review, titled *Transforming Defense: National Security in the 21st Century*, Report of the National Defense Panel, December 1997.[27]

Norris Review: A personal review of Army's school system by MG Frank Norris at the direction of General Westmoreland.[28]

Parker Panel: Ad hoc panel appointed by CSA General Westmoreland in 1969. It was headed by MG D. S. Parker. It studied institutional organization on the Army in the continental US, and reported 68 recommended changes in 1970.[29]

Patch-Simpson Board: Board of Officers on the Reorganization of the War Department created on 30 August 1945 by General Thomas T. Handy, Deputy Chief of Staff. It was first put under the direction of General Patch. When Patch died unexpectedly in November, the board fell under the direction of Lieutenant General William H. Simpson. The final report of the board was delivered to General Handy on 23 January 1946.[30]

PENTANA Study: A study conducted at the Army War College at the behest of Chief of Staff General Matthew Ridgway. Its full title was "Doctrinal and Organizational Concepts for Atomic-Nonatomic Army the Period 1960-1970." The study was completed in December 1955. It called for the creation of a small, 8,600-man division to replace the infantry, airborne, and armored divisions. The new division was to be completely air transportable, and sub-divided into five self-sufficient "battle groups." It encountered sufficient resistance from many within the Army's senior leadership, but was approved by Ridgway's successor, General Maxwell Taylor, on 1 June 1956 as a model for future research and development of weapons, equipment, and organization.[31]

Project SOLARIUM: A study of policy options conducted by three task forces. The task forces investigated modes of prosecuting the Cold War in the first year of the Eisenhower administration.[32]

Project 14: One-month study conducted by Brigadier General Colin Powell for incoming CSA General Wickhman that explored the direction to be taken by the Army in the coming four years. So named because it consisted of 14 officers.[33]

Quadrennial Defense Review: The first of the quadrennial reviews produced. Mandated by Congress in the Military Force Structure Review

Act of 1997, which was included in the annual National Defense Authorization Act for Fiscal Year 1997. The report was issued under the imprimatur of Secretary of Defense William Perry in May 1997.[34]

Quadrennial Defense Review:[35] (2001)

Quicksilver I & II: Follow-up studies to the Anteus force structure reduction study.[36]

RETO: Review of Education and Training of Officers, conducted during 1977-78.[37]

ROAD: Reorganization Objective Army Divisions (1961-1965).[38]

Rostow-Endicott Report: The Teaching of Strategy and Foreign Policy at Senior War Colleges. A personal assessment of the aforementioned conducted by Eugene V. Rostow at the behest of Secretary of Defense Caspar Weinberger. Rostow was assisted in preparing the report by Dr. John E. Endicott, the Director of the Institute for National Strategic Studies at the National Defense University. The study was initiated in February 1986 and the final report was transmitted to Weinberger on 11 June 1987.[39]

STEADFAST Reorganization: A study initiated in late 1971 to study the reorganization of the Continental Army Command. Assistant Vice Chief of Staff Lieutenant General William E. DePuy and a small group of officers with the office of Chief of Staff William Westmoreland were largely responsible for developing the reorganization plan. As a result of this study and its recommendations, a wide-ranging reorganization was announced by Secretary of the Army Froehlke and General Creighton W. Abrams on 11 January 1973. The 1973 reorganization resulted in the dissolution of the Continental Army Command and the Combat Developments Command. The functions of these two commands were then redistributed to two new commands, the United States Army Forces Command (FORSCOM) and the United States Army Training and Doctrine Command (TRADOC).[40]

Stillwell Report: "Army Activities in Underdeveloped Areas Short of Declared War," 13 October 1961.

A Study of Strategic Lessons Learned in Vietnam: Study conducted by the BDM Corporation for the Army War College in 1978-1979. Its findings were published in a massive, eight volume compendium in 1980. It was critical of the Army's ability to fight unconventional war. Its conclusions, however, were largely ignored. Instead the Army turned to the less controversial interpretations offered by Colonel Harry G. Summers, Jr. in *On Strategy: A Critical Analysis of the Vietnam War* (1982).

124

Total Force Study: Initiated in August 1973. Secretary of Defense acted on study recommendations in June 1975.[41]

Traub Committee: A committee appointed by CSA General George Decker to study the recommendations of the Hoelscher Committee. It was placed under the direction of Comptroller of the Army Lieutenant General David W. Traub. While the Traub Committee was carrying out its review, its work was partially overwhelmed by reorganization ideas proposed by the new Secretary of Defense, Robert McNamara.[42]

Williams Board: Officer Education and Training Review Board, chaired by CONARC deputy commander Lieutenant General Edward T. Williams. Convened in January 1958 and completed in July.[43]

Notes

1. Brooks E. Kleber, "The Army Looks At Its Need for Military History," *Military Affairs*, v.37, n.2 (April 1973), pp.47-48.

2. McCormick, *The Downsized Warrior*, p.34.

3. Thomas K. Adams, *The Army After Next: The First Postindustrial Army* (Westport, CT: Praeger, 2006).

4. Hewes, *From Root to McNamara*, pp.208-12.

5. This is a generic term for a class of board occasionally convened.

6. Hawkins and Carafano, *Prelude to Army XXI*, p.22.

7. Huba Wass de Czege, Final Report, Army Staff College Level Training Study, 13 June 1983, DTIC accession # ADA144852. Available at: http://handle.dtic.mil/100.2/ADA144852.

8. Harry G. Summers, *The Astarita Report: A Military Strategy for the Multipolar World* (Carlisle Barracks, PA: Strategic Studies Institute, US Army War College, 1981).

9. McCormick, *The Downsized Warrior*, pp.36-37, and Powell, *My American Journey*, pp.457-58. For a more in depth analysis, see Don M. Snider, *Strategy, Forces and Budgets: Dominant Influences in Executive Decision Making, Post-Cold War, 1989-91* (Carlisle, PA: Strategic Studies Institute, February 1993).

10. The Bottom-Up Review is available online at: http://www.fas.org/man/docs/bur/. See also McCormick, *The Downsized Warrior*, pp.39-51.

11. John P. White, et. al. *Directions for Defense: Report of the Commission on Roles and Missions of the Armed Forces* (Washington, DC: US Government Printing Office, 2005).

12. DOD FOIA, Ref. 95-F-1939. Secretary of Defense William Perry to Senator Strom Thurmond, re: Perry's comments on the report of the Commission on Roles and Missions of the Armed Forces, 24 August 1995. Available at: http://www.dod.mil/pubs/foi/other/.

13. Chapman, *The Origins and Development of the National Training Center 1976-1984*, p.7.

14. Ball, *On Responsible Command* (1983), pp.413-14.

15. Hewes, *From Root to McNamara*, pp.223-31.

16. DOD FOIA, available at: http://www.dod.mil/pubs/foi/dsb/.

17. The copy used for this project is a reproduction, bound together with the "The Teaching of Strategy and Foreign Policy at the Senior War Colleges: A Personal Assessment" and "The Clements Committee Report" available in the Combined Arms Research Library, Dewey call number 355.0711 T531 1987.

18. Ball, *On Responsible Command*, p.270f.

19. Ibid., p.261f.

20. Ibid., p.370f.

21. Hewes, *From Root to McNamara*, pp.174-79.

22. Ibid., pp.316ff.

23. DDRS, 1998,F175-76, 1936.

24. See Ian Horwood, *Interservice Rivalry and Airpower in Vietnam* (Fort Leavenworth, KS: Combat Studies Institute, 2006), pp.30-47; Hamilton Howze, *A Cavalryman's Story: Memoirs of a Twentieth-Century Army General* (Washington, DC: Smithsonian Institution Press, 1996); Barbara A. Sorrill, *The Origins, Deliberations, and Recommendations of the U.S. Army Tactical Mobility Requirements Board* (Fort Leavenworth, KS: Combat Developments Center, 1969); J. A. Stockfisch, *The 1962 Howze Board and Army Combat Developments* (Santa Monica, CA: RAND, 1994); and Lieutenant General John J. Tolson, *Airmobility 1961-1971* (Washington, DC: Department of the Army, 1989.

25. Downie, *Learning from Conflict*, pp.75-77.

26. Yarrison, *The Modern Louisiana Maneuvers*, passim.

27. Available at: http://www.dtic.mil/ndp/FullDoc2.pdf.

28. Ball, *On Responsible Command*, p.433f.

29. Stewart, gen. ed., *American Military History*, v.II, p.385.

30. Hewes, *From Root to McNamara*, pp.146ff.

31. Wilson, *Maneuver and Firepower*, pp.270-71.

32. Dockrill, *Eisenhower's New Look National Security Program*, pp.33-35, and Immerman and Bowie, *Waging Peace*, pp.123-43.

33. Powell, *My American Journey*, p.279.

34. William S. Cohen, *Report of the Quadrennial Defense Review*, May 1997. Available at: http://www.dod.mil/pubs/qdr/.

35. Available at: http://www.dod.mil/pubs/qdr2001.pdf.

36. McCormick, *The Downsized Warrior*, p.34.

37. *A Review of Education and Training for Officers* (Washington, DC: Headquarters, Department of the Army, 30 June 1978). Available at: http://handle.dtic.mil/100.2/ADA070772. See also Ball, *Of Responsible Command*, pp.465-68, and *Department of the Army Historical Summary: FY 1978*, pp.29-30.

38. Wilson, *Maneuver and Firepower*, pp.293-314. For Secretary of Defense Robert S. McNamara's review of ROAD, reference NARA, RG 200, Records of Robert S. McNamara, Box 16.

39. Eugene V. Rostow and John E. Endicott, "The Teaching of Strategy and Foreign Policy at the Senior War Colleges: A Personal Assessment." The copy

126

used for this project is a reproduction, bound together with the "Senior Military Schools Review Board Report (Dougherty Board)" and "The Clements Committee Report" available in the Combined Arms Research Library, Dewey call number 355.0711 T531 1987.

40. James A. Bowden, *Operation STEADFAST: The United States Army Reorganizes Itself* (US Marine Corps Command and Staff College, April 1985). Available online at: http://www.globalsecurity.org/military/library/report/1985/BJA.htm. Also *Department of the Army Historical Summary: FY 1973*, p.44. Available online at: http://www.army.mil/cmh/html/bookshelves/collect/Department of the Army Historical Summary.html.

41. *Department of the Army Historical Summary: FY 1975*, pp.24-25.

42. Hewes, *From Root to McNamara*, pp.344-54.

43. Ball, *On Responsible Command*, p.336f.

Bibliography

Archival Sources

Combined Arms Center, Fort Leavenworth, Kansas.
Combined Arms Center History Office Working Files.
Combined Arms Doctrine Development, Office Files.

Dwight D. Eisenhower Library, Abilene, Kansas.
Dwight D. Eisenhower, Papers as President (Ann Whitman Files).
White House Office, Office of Special Assistant for National Security Affairs.
White House Office, Office of the Staff Secretary.

National Archives and Records Administration, College Park, Maryland.
Nixon Presidential Materials.
Record Group 200-Records of Robert S. McNamara.
Record Group 218-Records of the Joint Chiefs of Staff.

Nixon Presidential Library, Online
National Security Memoranda. Available at: http://www.nixonlibrary.gov/virtuallibrary/documents/nationalsecuritymemoranda.php.

Published Documents

Aspin, Les. *Report on the Bottom-Up Review*, October 1993. Available at: http://www.fas.org/man/docs/bur/.

The American Presidency Project [online]. Santa Barbara, CA: University of California (hosted), Gerhard Peters (database). Available at: http://www.presidency.ucsb.edu/ws/?pid=18731.

Cohen, William S. *Report of the Quadrennial Defense Review*, May 1997. Available at: http://www.dod.mil/pubs/qdr/index.html.

Declassified Documents Retrieval System. Microfiche Collection. (Available at the Combined Arms Research Library, Fort Leavenworth, Kansas).

Department of Defense, Freedom of Information Act (FOIA) Reading Room, http://www.dod.mil/pubs/foi/nato/.

Foreign Relations of the United States, 1950, vol.I. Washington, DC: US Government Printing Office.

Foreign Relations of the United States, 1952-1954, v.II: *National Security Policy*. Washington, DC: US Government Printing Office.

Foreign Relations of the United States, 1955-1957, v.IV: *Western European Security and Integration*. Washington, DC: US Government Printing Office, 1986.

Foreign Relations of the United States, 1961-1963, v.VII: *National Security Policy*. Washington, DC: US Government Printing Office.

Galambos, Louis, ed. *The Papers of Dwight David Eisenhower*, vol.XII: *NATO and the Campaign of 1952*. Baltimore, MD: the Johns Hopkins University Press, 1989.

Public Papers of the Presidents.

A Review of the Education and Training for Officers, 5 vols. Washington, DC: Headquarters, Department of the Army, 30 June 1978. Volume 1, which contains the executive summary, is available on DTIC, accession # ADA070772, at: http://handle.dtic.mil/100.2/ADA070772.

Ross, Stephen T., and David Alan Rosenberg, eds. *America's Plans for War Against the Soviet Union 1945-1950*, 15 vols. New York: Garland Publishing, 1989.

Rumsfeld, Donald. *Quadrennial Defense Review Report*, 30 September 2001. Washington, DC: Department of Defense, 2001.

Summers, Harry G., Jr. *The Astarita Report: A Military Strategy for a Multipolar World*. Carlisle Barracks, PA: US Army War College, 1981.

Wass de Czege, Huba. *Final Report, Army Staff College Level Training Study*, 13 June 1983, DTIC accession # ADA144852. Available at: http://handle.dtic.mil/100.2/ADA144852.

White, John P., et. al. *Directions for Defense: Report of the Commission on Roles and Missions of the Armed Forces*. Washington, DC: US Government Printing Office, 2005.

Official Histories

CAC History Office, *U.S. Army Combined Arms Center 1985 Annual Historical Review*. Fort Leavenworth, KS: US Army Combined Arms Center, 1986.

Cole, Alice C., et. al. *The Department of Defense: Documents on Establishment and Organization 1944-1978*. Washington, DC: Historical Office, Office of the Secretary of Defense, 1978.

Condit, Doris M. *History of the Office of the Secretary of Defense*, v.II: *The Test of War 1950-1953*. Washington, DC: Historical Office, Office of the Secretary of Defense, 1988.

Defense Threat Reduction Agency. *Defense's Nuclear Agency 1947-1997*. Washington, DC: US Department of Defense, 2002.

Department of the Army Historical Summary [Multiple years]. Available at: http://www.army.mil/cmh/html/bookshelves/collect/dahsum.html.

Hewes, James E., Jr. *From Root to McNamara: Army Organization and Administration 1900-1963*. Washington, DC: Center of Military History, 1975.

Lawrence S. Kaplan, et.al., *History of the Office of the Secretary of Defense*, vol. V: The *McNamara Ascendancy 1961-1965*. Washington, DC: Office of the Secretary of Defense, 2006.

Leighton, Richard M. *History of the Office of the Secretary of Defense*, v.III: *Strategy, Money, and the New Look 1953-1956*. Washington, DC: Office of the Secretary of Defense, 2001.

Poole, Walter S. *History of the Joint Chiefs of Staff, The Joint Chiefs of Staff and National Policy, v.IV: 1950-1952*. Washington, DC: Office of Joint History, 1998.

Rearden, Steven L. *History of the Office of the Secretary of Defense*, vol.I: *The Formative Years 1947-1950*. Washington, DC: Historical Office, Office of the Secretary of Defense, 1984.

Shrader, Charles R. *History of Operations Research in the United States Army*, vol.I: *1942-1962*. Washington, DC: Office of the Deputy Under Secretary of the Army for Operations Research, United States Army, 2006.

Watson, Robert J. *History of the Office of the Secretary of Defense*, vol.IV: *Into the Missile Age 1956-1960*. Washington, DC: Historical Office, Office of the Secretary of Defense, 1997.

Memoirs

Clark, Wesley K. *Waging Modern War*. New York: PublicAffairs, 2001.

Clinton, Bill. *My Life*. New York: Alfred A. Knopf, 2004.

Franks, Tommy. *American Soldier*, with Malcolm McConnell. New York: Regan Books, 2004.

Gavin, James M. *War and Peace in the Space Age*. New York: Harper & Brothers, 1958.

Howze, Hamilton. *A Cavalryman's Story: Memoirs of a Twentieth-Century Army General*. Washington, DC: Smithsonian Institution Press, 1996.

Kissinger, Henry. *White House Years*. Boston, MA: Little, Brown and Company, 1979.

Nitze, Paul. *From Hiroshima to Glasnost: At the Center of Decision, A Memoir*. New York: Grove Weidenfeld, 1989.

Powell, Colin L. *My American Journey*, with Joseph E. Persico. New York: Random House, 1995.

Radford, Arthur. *From Pearl Harbor to Vietnam: The Memoirs of Arthur Radford*, edited by Stephen J. Jurika, Jr. Stanford, CA: Hoover Institute Press, 1980.

Ridgway, Matthew B. *Soldier: The Memoirs of Matthew B. Ridgway*. New York: Harper & Brothers, 1956.

Schwartzkopf, H. Norman. *It Doesn't Take a Hero*. New York: Linda Grey Bantam Books, 1992.

Taylor, Maxwell D. *Swords and Plowshares: A Memoir*. New York: De Capo Press, 1972.

Westmoreland, William C. *A Soldier Reports*. Garden City, NY: Doubleday, 1976.

Newspapers and Journals

Armed Forces Management

Armor

Army

Chicago Tribune

Christian Science Monitor

Military Review

New York Times

Parameters

Washington Post

Secondary Sources

Association of the United States Army. *Goldwater-Nichols Department of Defense Reorganization Act of 1986-A Primer*. Arlington, VA: Association of the United States Army, 1988.

Bacevich, A. J. "The Paradox of Professionalism: Eisenhower, Ridgway, and the Challenge to Civilian Control, 1953-1955," *The Journal of Military History*, v.61, n.2 (April 1997).

_____. *The Pentomic Era: The US Army Between Korea and Vietnam*. Washington, DC: National Defense University Press, 1986.

Ball, Harry P. *Of Responsible Command: A History of the U.S. Army War College*, revised edition. Carlisle Barracks, PA: Alumni Association of the US Army War College, 1994.

Bassford, Christopher. *Clausewitz in English: The Reception of Clausewitz in Britain and America, 1815-1945*. New York: Oxford University Press, 1994.

Baumann, Robert F., and Lawrence A. Yates, with Versalle F. Washington, *"My Clan Against the World": US and Coalition Forces in Somalia 1992-1994.* Fort Leavenworth, KS: Combat Studies Institute Press, 2004.

BDM Corporation, *A Study of Strategic Lessons Learned in Vietnam,* 8 vols. 1979-80.

Binder, James L. *Lemnitzer: A Soldier for His Time.* Washington, DC: Brassey's, 1997.

Birtle, Andrew J. *U.S. Army Counterinsurgency and Contingency Operations Doctrine 1942-1976.* Washington, DC: Center of Military History, United States Army, 2006.

Borowski, Harry R. *A Hollow Threat: Air Power and Containment before Korea.* Westport, CT: Greenwood Press, 1982.

Bowie, Robert R., and Richard H. Immerman. *Waging Peace: How Eisenhower Shaped an Enduring Cold War Strategy.* New York: Oxford University Press, 1998.

Bowden, Mark. *Black Hawk Down: A Story of Modern War.* New York: Atlantic Monthly, 1999.

Bowden, James A. *Operation STEADFAST: The United States Army Reorganizes Itself.* Quantico, VA: USMC Command and Staff College, 1985. Available online at: http://www.globalsecurity.org/military/library/report/1985/BJA.htm.

Bundy, William. *A Tangled Web: The Making of Foreign Policy in the Nixon Presidency.* New York: Hill and Wang, 1998.

Chapman, Anne W. *The Army's Training Revolution 1973-1990: An Overview.* TRADOC Historical Studies Series.

_____. *The National Training Center Matures 1985-1993.* Fort Monroe, VA: Military History Office, United States Army Training and Doctrine Command, 1997.

_____. *The Origins and Development of the National Training Center 1976-1984.* TRADOC Historical Monograph Series. Fort Monroe, VA: Office of the Command Historian, United States Army Training and Doctrine Command, 1992.

_____. et. al. *Prepare the Army for War: A Historical Overview of the Army Training and Doctrine Command 1973-1998*. Fort Monroe, VA: Military History Office, United States Army Training and Doctrine Command, 1998.

Cochran, Thomas D., William M. Arkin, and Milton M. Hoenig. *Nuclear Weapons Databook*, vol.I: *U.S. Nuclear Forces and Capabilities*. Cambridge, MA: Ballinger Publishing, 1984.

Coffman, Edward M. "The Course of Military History in the United States Since World War II," *The Journal of Military History*, v.61, n.4 (October 1997), pp.761-75.

Conn, Stetson *Historical Work in the United States Army, 1862-1954*. Washington, DC: United States Army, Center of Military History, 1980.

Cosmas, Graham A. *MACV: The Joint Command in the Years of Escalation 1962-1967*. Washington, DC: Center of Military History, United States Army, 2006.

Crane, Conrad C. *Avoiding Vietnam: The US Army's Response to Defeat in Southeast Asia*. Carlisle, PA: Strategic Studies Institute, Army War College, September 2002.

Daalder, Ivo H. *The Nature and Practice of Flexible Response: NATO Strategy and Theater Nuclear Forces Since 1967*. New York: Columbia University Press, 1991.

Dallek, Robert. *Nixon and Kissinger: Partners in Power*. New York: HarperCollins, 2007.

Dastrup, Boyd L. *The US Army Command and General Staff College: A Centennial History*. Manhattan, KS: Sunflower University Press, 1982.

Davidson, Phillip B. *Vietnam at War: The History 1946-1975*. New York: Oxford University Press, 1991.

Dockrill, Saki. *Eisenhower's New-Look National Security Policy, 1953-1961.* Basingstoke, England: Macmillan Press, 1996.

Doughty, Robert A. *The Evolution of US Army Tactical Doctrine, 1946-1976.* Leavenworth Papers. Fort Leavenworth, KS: Combat Studies Institute Press, 1979.

Downie, Richard Duncan. *Learning from Conflict: The U.S. Military in Vietnam, El Salvador, and the Drug War.* Westport, CT: Praeger, 1998.

Duffield, John S. *Power Rules: The Evolution of NATO's Conventional Force Posture.* Stanford, CA: Stanford University Press, 1995.

Dunnigan, James F., and Raymond Macedonia. *Getting it Right: American Military Reforms after Vietnam to the Persian Gulf and Beyond.* New York: William Morrow, 1993.

Dupuy, Trevor N. *A Genius for War: The German Army General Staff, 1807-1945.* Englewood Cliffs, NJ: Prentice-Hall, 1977.

Echevarria, Antulio J., II. *Imagining Future War: The West's Technological Revolution and Visions of Wars to Come, 1880-1914.* Westport, CT: Praeger Security International, 2007.

Elliot, David C. "Project Vista and Nuclear Weapons in Europe," *International Security,* v.11, n.1 (Summer 1986), pp.163-83.

Erdmann, Andrew P. N. "War no longer has any logic whatever: Dwight D. Eisenhower and the thermonuclear revolution" in *Cold War Statesmen Confront the Bomb: Nuclear Diplomacy since 1945,* edited by John Lewis Gaddis, et. al. Oxford: Oxford University Press, 1999.

Fautua, David T. "The 'Long Pull' Army: NSC 68, the Korean War, and the Creation of the Cold War US Army," *The Journal of Military History,* v.61, n.1 (January 1997).

Feickert, Andrew. *US Army's Modular Redesign: Issues for Congress.* Washington, DC: Congressional Research Service, 2006.

Flournoy, Michéle A., et. al. *Report of the National Defense University Qua-*

drennial Defense Review 2001 Working Group. Washington, DC: Institute for National Strategic Studies, National Defense University, November 2000.

Franks, Frederick M., Jr. *Battle Labs: Maintaining the Edge*. Fort Monroe, VA: Headquarters, US Army Training and Doctrine Command, May 1994.

Freedman, Lawrence. *The Evolution of Nuclear Strategy*, 2nd edn. New York: St. Martin's Press, 1989.

Gabel, Christopher R. *The U.S. Army GHQ Maneuvers of 1941*. Washington, DC: Center of Military History, 1991.

Garthoff, Raymond L. *Détente and Confrontation: American-Soviet Relations from Nixon to Reagan*. Washington, DC: The Brookings Institution, 1985.

Gavin, Francis J. "The Myth of Flexible Response: United States Strategy in Europe during the 1960s," *The International History Review*, XXIII, 4 (December 2001) 847-75.

Geelhoed, E. Bruce. *Charles E. Wilson and Controversy at the Pentagon, 1953-1957*. Detroit MI: Wayne State University Press, 1979.

Gray, Colin S. "What RAND Hath Wrought," *Foreign Policy*, n.4 (Fall 1971), pp.111-29.

Griffith, Robert K. *The U.S. Army's Transition to the All-Volunteer Force, 1968-1974*. Washington, DC: US Army Center of Military History, 1997.

Halberstam, David. *War in a Time of Peace: Bush, Clinton, and the Generals*. New York: Simon and Schuster, 2001.

Hanhimäki, Jussi. *The Flawed Architect: Henry Kissinger and American Foreign Policy*. New York: Oxford University Press, 2004.

Hattendorf, John B. *The Evolution of the U.S. Navy's Maritime Strategy 1977-1986*, Newport Paper 19. Newport, RI: Naval War College, 2004.

_____. *Sailors and Scholars: The Centennial History of the United States Naval War College*. Newport, RI: Naval War College Press, 1984.

Hawkins, Glen R., and James Jay Carafano. *Prelude to Army XXI: U.S. Army Division Design Initiatives and Experiments 1917-1995*. Washington, DC: Center of Military History, 1997.

Heller, Charles E., and Elizabeth R. Snoke. *CSI Historical Bibliography No.1: The Integrated Battlefield 1945-1965*. Fort Leavenworth, KS: Combat Studies Institute, July 1980. Available at: http://www.cgsc.army.mil/carl/resources/csi/heller2/heller2.asp.

Herbert, Paul H. *Deciding What Has to Be Done: General William E. DePuy and the 1976 Edition of FM 100-5, Operations*. Leavenworth Papers, no.16. Fort Leavenworth: Combat Studies Institute, 1988.

Herring, George C. *America's Longest War: The United States and Vietnam, 1950-1975*, 3rd edn. New York: McGraw Hill, 1996.

Howard, Michael. "The Relevance of Traditional Strategy," *Foreign Affairs*, v.51, n.2 (January 1973), pp.253-66.

Hunt, Michael H. *The American Ascendancy: How the United States Gained & Wielded Global Dominance*. Chapel Hill, NC: University of North Carolina Press, 2007.

Kaiser, David E. *American Tragedy: Kennedy, Johnson, and the Origins of the Vietnam War*. Cambridge, MA: Belknap Press of Harvard University Press, 2000.

Kagan, Frederick W. *Finding the Target: The Transformation of American Military Policy*. New York: Encounter Books, 2006.

Kitfield, James. *Prodigal Soldiers: How the Generation of Officers Born of Vietnam Revolutionized the American Style of War*. New York: Simon & Schuster, 1995.

Kunz, Diane B. *Butter and Guns: America's Cold War Economic Diplomacy*. New York: The Free Press, 1997.

Laird, Melvin R. "Iraq: Learning the Lessons of Vietnam," *Foreign Affairs*. November/December 2005.

138

Leffler, Melvin A. *Preponderance of Power: National Security, the Truman administration, and the Cold War*. Stanford, CA: Stanford University Press, 1992.

Linn, Brian McAlister. *The Echo of Battle: The Army's Way of War*. Cambridge, MA: Harvard University Press, 2007.

Lock-Pullan, Richard. "'An Inward Looking Time': The United States Army, 1973-1976," *The Journal of Military History*, v.67, n.2 (April 2003), pp.483-511.

_____. *U.S. Army Innovation and American Strategic Culture after Vietnam*. London: Routledge, 2006.

Logevall, Fredrik. *Choosing War: The Lost Chance for Peace and the Escalation of War in Vietnam*. Berkeley, CA: University of California Press, 1999.

Macgregor, Douglas A. *Transformation Under Fire: Revolutionizing How America Fights*. Westport, CT: Praeger, 2003.

Mann, James. *Rise of the Vulcans: The History of Bush's War Cabinet*. New York: Viking, 2004.

Mataxis, Theodore C., and Seymour L. Goldberg, *Nuclear Tactics, Weapons, and Firepower in the Pentomic Division, Battle Group, and Company*. Harrisburg, PA: The Military Service Publishing Company, 1958.

May, Ernest R., ed. *American Cold War Strategy: Interpreting NSC 68*. Boston MA: Bedford Books, 1993.

McCormick, David. *The Downsized Warrior: America's Army in Transition*. New York: New York University Press, 1998.

McGrath, John J. *The Brigade: A History, Its Organization and Employment in the US Army*. Fort Leavenworth, KS: Combat Studies Institute Press, 2004.

_____. *The Other End of the Spear: The Tooth-to-Tail Ratio (T3R) in Modern Military Operations*. Fort Leavenworth, KS: Combat Studies Institute Press, 2007.

_____. gen. ed., *An Army at War: Change in the Midst of Conflict.* The Proceedings of the Combat Studies Institute 2005 Military History Symposium. Fort Leavenworth, KS: Combat Studies Institute Press, August 2005.

McMaster, H. R. *Dereliction of Duty: Lyndon Johnson, Robert McNamara, the Joint Chiefs of Staff, and the Lies That Led to Vietnam.* New York: Harper-Collins, 1997.

Meinhart, Richard. *Strategic Planning by the Chairmen, Joint Chiefs of Staff, 1990-2005.* Carlisle, PA: Strategic Studies Institute, April 2006.

Metz, Steven. *American Strategy: Issues and Alternatives for the Quadrennial Defense Review.* Carlisle, PA: Strategic Studies Institute, September 2000.

_____. "Eisenhower and the Planning of American Grand Strategy," *Journal of Strategic Studies*, v.14 (March 1991), pp.49-71.

_____. *Eisenhower as Strategist: The Coherent Use of Power in War and Peace.* Carlisle, PA: Strategic Studies Institute, US Army War College, 1993.

_____. ed. *Revising the Two MTW Force Shaping Paradigm.* Carlisle, PA: Strategic Studies Institute, April 2001.

_____. and James Kievit, *Strategy and the Revolution in Military Affairs: From Theory to Policy.* Carlisle, PA: Strategic Studies Institute, 1995.

Mitchell, George C. *Matthew B. Ridgway: Soldier, Statesman, Scholar, Citizen.* Mechanicsburg, PA: Stackpole Books, 2002.

Moenk, Jean R. *Operation STEADFAST Historical Summary: A History of the Reorganization of the U.S. Continental Army Command (1972-1973).* Fort McPherson, GA: Headquarters, US Army Forces Command, 1974.

Murray, Williamson, ed. *Army Transformation: A View from the U.S. Army War College.* Carlisle, PA: Strategic Studies Institute, July 2001.

Palmer, Michael. *Origins of the Maritime Strategy: The Development of American Naval Strategy 1945-1955.* Annapolis, MD: Naval Institute Press, 1988.

Pfaltzgraff, Robert L., Jr., and Richard H. Shultz, Jr. *The United States Army: Challenges and Missions for the 1990s*. Lexington, MA: Lexington Books, 1991.

Pickett, William B. *Dwight David Eisenhower and American Power*. Wheeling, IL: Harlan Davidson, 1995.

Reinhardt, G. C., and W. R. Kintner. *Atomic Weapons in Land Combat*. Harrisburg, PA: The Military Service Publishing Co., 1953.

Romjue, John L. *American Army Doctrine for the Post-Cold War World*. Fort Monroe, VA: Military History Office, United States Training and Doctrine Command, 1997.

_____. *The Army of Excellence: The Development of the 1980s Army*. Fort Monroe, VA: Office of the Command Historian, United States Army Training and Doctrine Command, 1993.

_____. *From Active Defense to AirLand Battle: The Development of Army Doctrine 1973-1982*. Fort Monroe, VA: Historical Office, United States Army Training and Doctrine Command, 1984.

Rose, John P. *The Evolution of U.S. Army Nuclear Doctrine, 1945-1980*. Boulder, CO: Westview Press, 1980.

Rosenberg, David Alan. "The Origins of Overkill: Nuclear Weapons and American Strategy, 1945-1960," *International Security*, v.7, n.4 (Spring 1983), pp.3-71.

Ross, Steven T. *American War Plans 1945-1950*. New York: Garland Publishing, 1988.

Sagan, Scott D. *Moving Targets: Nuclear Strategy and National Security*. Princeton, NJ: Princeton University Press, 1989.

Scales, Robert H., Jr. *Certain Victory: The US Army in the Gulf War*. Washington, DC: US Government Printing Office, 1993.

Schulzinger, Robert D. *A Time for War: The United States and Vietnam, 1941-1975*. New York: Oxford University Press, 1997.

Schwartz, Hans-Peter. *Konrad Adenauer,* vol.2: *The Statesman, 1952-1967,* trans. by Geoffrey Penny. Providence, RI: Berghahn Books, 1991.

Schwartz, Thomas A. *Lyndon Johnson and Europe: In the Shadow of Vietnam.* Cambridge, MA: Harvard University Press, 2003.

Sepp, Kalev I. "The Pentomic Puzzle: The Influence of Personality on U.S. Army Organization 1952-1958," *Army History* (Winter 2001), pp.1-14.

Sherry, Michael S. *The Rise of American Air Power: The Creation of Armageddon.* New Haven, CT: Yale University Press, 1987.

Sixty Years of Reorganizing for Combat: A Historical Trends Analysis. Fort Leavenworth, KS: Combat Studies Institute, 1999.

Small, Melvin. *The Presidency of Richard Nixon.* Lawrence, KS: University Press of Kansas, 1999.

Smith, Rupert. *The Utility of Force: The Art of War in the Modern World.* New York: Alfred A. Knopf, 2005.

Snider, Don M. *Strategy, Forces and Budgets: Dominant Influences in Executive Decision Making, Post-Cold War, 1989-91.* Carlisle, PA: Strategic Studies Institute, February 1993.

Sorley, Lewis. *Reserve Forces in the Contingency Era: Issues and Answers.* Arlington, VA: 1993.

_____. *Thunderbolt: General Creighton Abrams and the Army of His Times.* New York: Simon and Schuster, 1992.

Soutor, Kevin. "To Stem the Red Tide: The German Report Series and Its Effect on American Defense Doctrine, 1948-1954," *The Journal of Military History*, v.57, n.4 (October 1993), pp.653-688.

Sparrow, John C. *History of Personnel Demobilization in the United States Army.* Washington, DC: Center of Military History, facsimile edition, 1994.

Spiller, Roger J. "In the Shadow of the Dragon: Doctrine and the US Army after Vietnam," *RUSI Journal*, v.142, n.6 (December 1997), pp.41-54.

142

_____. _"Not War But Like War": The American Intervention in Lebanon_. Fort Leavenworth, KS: Combat Studies Institute, 1981.

_____. "War History and the History Wars: Establishing the Combat Studies Institute," _The Public Historian_, v.10, n.4 (Fall 1998), pp.65-81.

Stanton, Shelby L. _The Rise and Fall of an American Army_. Novato, CA: Presidio Press, 1985.

Stewart, Richard, gen. ed. _American Military History_, vol.II: _The United States Army in a Global Era, 1917-2003_. Washington, DC: Center of Military History, 2005.

Strachan, Hew. "Essay and Reflection: On Total War and Modern War," _The International History Review_, v.XXII, n.2 (June 2000), pp.341-70.

Stromseth, Jane E. _The Origins of Flexible Response: NATO's Debate Over Strategy in the 1960s_. Basingstoke, England: Macmillan Press, 1988.

Summers, Harry G., Jr. _The New World Strategy: A Military Policy for America's Future_. New York: Simon & Schuster, 1995.

_____. _On Strategy: A Critical Analysis of the Vietnam War_. New York: Dell Publishing, 1982.

_____. _On Strategy II: A Critical Analysis of the Gulf War_. New York: Dell Publishing, 1992.

Suri, Jeremi. _Henry Kissinger and the American Century_. Cambridge, MA: Belknap Press, 2007.

Taylor, Maxwell D. _The Uncertain Trumpet_. New York: Harper & Brothers, 1959.

Thompson, W. Scott, and Donaldson D. Frizze. _The Lessons of Vietnam_. New York: Crane, Russak & Company, 1977.

Tolson, John J. _Airmobility 1961-1971_. Washington, DC: Department of the Army, 1989.

Trachtenberg, Marc. "Strategic Thought in America, 1952-1966," *Political Science Quarterly*, v.104, n.2 (Summer 1989), pp.301-34.

Vetock, Dennis J. *Lessons Learned: A History of US Army Lesson Learning*. Carlisle Barracks, PA: US Army Military History Institute, 1988.

Weigley, Russell. *History of the United States Army*, rev. edn. Bloomington, IN: University of Indiana Press, 1984.

Williams, Phil. *The Senate and US Troops in Europe*. New York: St. Martin's Press, 1985.

Wohlstetter, Roberta. *Pearl Harbor: Warning and Decision*. Stanford, CA: Stanford University Press, 1962.

Woodward, Bob. *Bush at War*. New York: Simon and Schuster Paperbacks, 2002.

Yaqub, Salim. *Containing Arab Nationalism: The Eisenhower Doctrine in the Middle East*. Chapel Hill, NC: University of North Caroline Press, 2004.

Yarrison, James L. *The Modern Louisiana Maneuvers*. Washington, DC: Center of Military History, 1999.

Dissertations and Unpublished Papers

Bolles, Charles DeVallon Dugas. "The Search for an American Strategy: The Origins of the Kennedy Doctrine, 1936-1961." PhD Dissertation, University of Wisconsin, 1985.

Hanson, Thomas E. "America's First Cold War Army: Combat Readiness in the Eighth U.S. Army, 1949-1950." PhD Dissertation, Ohio State University, 2006.

Herbert, Paul Hardy. "Toward the Best Available thought: The Writing of Field Manual 100-5, 'Operations' by the United States Army 1973-1976." PhD Dissertation, Ohio State University, 1985.

Jussel, Paul C. "Intimidating the World: The United States Atomic Army, 1956-1960." PhD Dissertation, Ohio State University, 2004. Available at:

http://www.ohiolink.edu/etd/send- pdf.cgi/Jussel%20Paul%20C.pdf?acc_
num=osu1085083063.

Sheehan, Kevin P. "Preparing for an Imaginary War?: Examining Peacetime
Functions and Changes of Army Doctrine." PhD Dissertation, Harvard
University, 1988.

Trauschweizer, Ingo W. "Creating Deterrence for Limited War: The US Army
and the Defense of West Germany, 1953-1982." PhD Dissertation, University of Maryland, 2006. Available at: https://drum.umd.edu/dspace/bit-
stream/1903/3390/1/umi-umd-3202.pdf.